FOUL DEEDS AND SUSPICIOUS
DEATHS IN AND AROUND HALIFAX

TRUE CRIME FROM WHARNCLIFFE
Foul Deeds and Suspicious Deaths Series

Barking, Dagenham and
   Chadwell Heath
Barnet, Finchley and Hendon
Barnsley
Bath
Bedford
Birmingham
Black Country
Blackburn and Hyndburn
Bolton
Bradford
Brighton
Bristol
Cambridge
Cardiff
Carlisle
Chesterfield
Colchester
Cotswolds
Coventry
Crewe
Croydon
Cumbria
Derby
Doncaster
Dublin
Durham
Ealing
Fens
Folkestone and Dover

Glasgow
Grimsby and Cleethorpes
Guernsey
Guildford
Halifax
Hampstead, Holburn and
   St Pancras
Huddersfield
Hull
Isle of Wight
Islington
Jersey
Kensington and Chelsea
Leeds
Leicester
Lewisham and Deptford
Liverpool
London's East End
London's West End
Manchester
Mansfield
More Foul Deeds Barnsley
More Foul Deeds Birmingham
More Foul Deeds Chesterfield
More Foul Deeds Wakefield
Newcastle
Newport
Norfolk
Northampton
Nottingham

Oxfordshire
Pontefract and Castleford
Portsmouth
Reading
Richmond and Kingston
Rochdale
Rotherham
Scunthorpe
Sheffield
Shrewsbury and Around
   Shropshire
South Yorkshire
Southampton
Southend-on-Sea
Southport
Staffordshire and the Potteries
Stratford and South
   WarwickshireSuffolk
Swansea
Tees
The Fens
Uxbridge
Wakefield
Warwickshire
West Riding of Yorkshire
Wigan
Worcester
York
Yorkshire Coast

OTHER TRUE CRIME BOOKS FROM WHARNCLIFFE

Black Barnsley
Brighton Crime and Vice 1800–2000
Britain's Most Notorious Hangmen
Crafty Crooks and Conmen
Criminal Women
DNA Crime Investigations
Durham Executions
Enemies of the State
Essex Murders
Executions & Hangings in Newcastle & Morpeth
Great Hoaxers, Artful Fakers and Cheating Charlatans
Great Train Crimes
Hanged in Lancashire
Kent Murder and Mayhem
Jack the Ripper: Quest for a Killer
Miscarriages of Justice
Murder and Mayhem in North London
Norfolk Mayhem and Murder
Norwich Murders
Notorious Murders of the Twentieth Century
Rotherham Murders
Scotland Yards's Ghost Squad
Serial Killers: Butchers and Cannibals

Serial Killers: Murder Without Mercy
Serial Killers: The World's Most Evil
Strangeways: A Century of Hangings in Manchester
The A-Z of London Murders
The Guv'nors
The Plot to Kill Lloyd George
The Romford Outrage
The Sweeney
The Thames Torso Murders
The Wharncliffe A-Z of Yorkshire Murder
Unsolved East Anglian Murders
Unsolved London Murders: The 1920s and 1930s
Unsolved London Murders: The 1940s and 1950s
Unsolved Murders in and Around Derbyshire
Unsolved Murders in Victorian & Edwardian London
Unsolved Norfolk Murders
Unsolved Yorkshire Murders
War Crimes
Warwickshire's Murderous Women
Yorkshire's Hangmen
Yorkshire's Multiple Killers
Yorkshire's Murderous Women

Please contact us via any of the methods below for more information or a catalogue
WHARNCLIFFE BOOKS
47 Church Street, Barnsley, South Yorkshire, S70 2AS
Tel: 01226 734555 • 734222 • Fax: 01226 734438
email: enquiries@pen-and-sword.co.uk
website: www.wharncliffebooks.co.uk

Foul Deeds and Suspicious Deaths in and around
HALIFAX

STEPHEN WADE

Series Editor
Brian Elliott

Wharncliffe Books

First published in Great Britain in 2004
and reprinted in 2011 by
WHARNCLIFFE BOOKS
An imprint of
Pen & Sword Books Ltd
47 Church Street
Barnsley
South Yorkshire
S70 2AS

Copyright © Stephen Wade, 2004, 2011

ISBN 978 1 90342 545 9

Printed and bound in England
By CPI UK

Pen & Sword Books Ltd incorporates the Imprints of Pen & Sword Aviation,
Pen & Sword Family History, Pen & Sword Maritime, Pen & Sword Military,
Pen & Sword Discovery, Wharncliffe Local History, Wharncliffe True Crime,
Wharncliffe Transport, Pen & Sword Select, Pen & Sword Military Classics, Leo Cooper,
The Praetorian Press, Remember When, Seaforth Publishing and Frontline Publishing

For a complete list of Pen & Sword titles please contact
PEN & SWORD BOOKS LIMITED
47 Church Street, Barnsley, South Yorkshire, S70 2AS, England
E-mail: enquiries@pen-and-sword.co.uk
Website: www.pen-and-sword.co.uk

Contents

6

Introduction

After spending many hours looking through old newspapers, works by antiquarians, local histories from the various corners of the parish of Halifax, I have to explain the resulting reflections as again a confirmation of the stunning and enigmatic nature of murder in human communities. This is an easy conclusion to reach after reading such cases as that of Frederick Brett in 1889. Brett, a railway worker, in a drunken state, suspected his wife of infidelity, and slit her throat with a small pen-knife. When Brett was arrested, he simply said that he was 'only playing at Jack the Ripper.'

This was one more of those pathetic 'copy-cat' crimes, we might think. But murder cases are never that simple, because they are often the outcome of a long and painful failure either in a particular relationship or in the impossibility of an individual to know him or herself honestly. As Shakespeare said of King Lear in his destructive folly: 'He hath ever but slenderly known himself.' These sad cases of killings outside public houses, men possessed by jealousy, or murders done for a few pounds mostly have these human stories, with the same appeal to the reader as that of crime fiction.

The sources of these stories in Halifax have been difficult to find, but that is part of the pleasure of writing True Crime. The normal source is in the inquest books of coroners; yet in the case of Halifax parish, the West Riding coroner, Thomas Taylor, did not record anything. It seems to be an area overlooked in this context. However, Halifax is rich in another source for historiography: it has a thriving Antiquarian Society and a host of amateur historians with a profound local pride and a strong interest in the industrial and social history of Calderdale.

Is Halifax an unusually murderous place? No more than any other Yorkshire town burgeoning during the heyday of the Industrial Revolution. But most people will be familiar with the old saying: 'From Hell, Hull and Halifax, Good Lord deliver us.' Halifax is there in that alliterative statement largely because of the Gibbet. As the editor of a journal in Victorian times said, 'The list of executions under the Gibbet Law at Halifax was … so formidable that there is no reason to wonder at the proverbial petition of thieves and vagabonds.'

The town has its dark and dismal topography, as do all West Riding towns with so much industrial history; it abounds in alleys, courts, ginnels and garths – places that a modern sociologist might define as being lacking in 'defensible space'. In other words, there are places with really menacing atmosphere, and these clearly proliferated as industrial and commercial premises were squeezed into these tight valleys. As you drive into Halifax from the M62 near Huddersfield, you pass Southowram, and see the huge hilly ridge on your right, with isolated farmhouses and distant dwellings, reminding you that Emily Bronte's *Wuthering Heights* was set just a few valleys away to the north.

Even in legends going back to the medieval period, violence is associated with the place: one story of the origin of the name includes 'a certain evil clerk who cut off the head of a saintly maiden, and hung it on a yew tree, where it was greatly revered. The fibres beneath the bark of the tree were held to be the long hair of the maiden, and pilgrims visited the yew, calling it 'holy hair.' By Victorian years, the hard and extreme acts of punishment maintain this tough image: John Turner was tried at York and transported for ten years; Mary Thompson, aged twenty-one, was put away for ten years for robbing a Leeds man of seven shillings and sixpence. Poor Martin Maguire was transported for fourteen years for burglary.

But, despite the desperate social problems of these earlier times, and the forbidding geography around the town, Calderdale is very beautiful. Phyllis Bentley, the famous novelist, wrote a long essay on 'Romantic Halifax' and mentions an old statement that Halifax people were 'rude and arrogant', only to displace this with an insistence that it is lovely country, with 'sweeping, interlocking hills, narrow winding valleys, sloping fields of rough grass…' When William Wordsworth's sister, Dorothy, was in the town in the 1780s,

Robert Gittings notes that 'Halifax was still a country town, the first worsted mill was not opened until 1787 and the population at the 1801 Census was still under nine thousand...'

However, when that acceleration of industry and population happened, it certainly created the kinds of social problems which engender crime, and that crime is often violent. *The Halifax Courier* and *Halifax Guardian*, my main sources, tell tragic tales of suicides, muggings, riots and open verdicts. Here, the historian finds blurred, dark images of people leading hard, exhausting lives in the proletariat: their lives were a round of working, drinking and trying to raise their families. Many of the stories from the period c.1840–1900 are embedded in these working lives, where people worked ten to twelve hours a day; where women often took in sewing or washing to keep the family income up to the necessary level.

Having said this, the narratives here also reflect a certain thread of adventure and romance; there were highwaymen, with crepe across their faces, like the men who robbed 'two foreign gentlemen' near Halifax in 1780 and 'robbed him of his purse' or the story of the revenge killings in fourteeth century Elland, told and retold by writers through the centuries. Then, of course, the most notorious murder in Halifax in the pre-twentieth century period: the Cragg Vale Coiners' killing of the lawman who came after them in their high fastness.

In common with most West Riding towns and villages, there has always been a spirit of local pride even at the level of a small settlement within the parish as a whole. For instance, as a directory of 1838 makes clear, these oppositions were profoundly important in the case of Halifax: 'Elland... had also a cloth hall, and for a long period maintained a rivalry with Halifax, being the only chartered market-town in the parish.' And the writer goes on to locate divisions in identity and community going back to the reign of Edward III: 'The Saviles... when their male line became extinct, in consequence of a deadly quarrel with the Beaumonts, Quarmbys and Lockwoods.' (see chapter 1)

In commenting on the bulk of the material for this book, it soon becomes apparent that Halifax has been entirely typical of the divisive class conflicts of the new industrial town sprouting in the mid-Victorian prosperity. As was the case famously with Frederick Engels' account of Manchester, here in Halifax the road out to Lancashire through King Cross splits an area of heavy industrialisation and the grandeur and open space of Savile Park, with Wainhouse Folly as some kind of symbolic edifice, asserting the middle class aspirations of a town so proud of its Literary and Philosophical Society and Thespians.

The criminal history of the town and surrounding conurbations, then, is one of a dynamic mix: some extreme crimes against the person and property committed by the rootless shifting labour force; some sophisticated frauds in the world of commerce, and perhaps most frequent of all, the violent crimes done within the family. A common headline across the years is something like 'Wife Stabbed by Distracted Husband.' Today, we might look for stress in the workplace, genetic factors, Asperger's Syndrome etc. But in 1850 you were a killer-end of story.

For all these reasons, a brief history of murder and suspicious deaths in Halifax throws light on the social history of a significant period in British history. In research of this kind, the historian begins to notice patterns and causes. For instance, in the newspaper reports for the period c.1890–1910 the number of suicides of young women was alarmingly high, and other sources confirm this. *The Gentleman's Magazine* a century before records a high number of young female suicides in the South Yorkshire area. In the case of Halifax, reasons could easily be found, mostly moral and religious, linked to the shame of illegitimacy.

Finally, Halifax has its links to crimes which form part of the standard works on murder: Peter Sutcliffe, The Yorkshire Ripper, killed a young girl near a bus-stop on Savile Park. Christie of 10 Rillington Place, was Halifax-born. I have included brief accounts of these, as readers with an interest in criminal history would expect this. The crimes in the years c.1950–1970 have their local mythology or urban myths, and this oral history has been an intriguing part of the work done. For instance, I heard several people tell stories about a man in a car, in female attire and with a hammer by his side, seen in a car park at the time of the Yorkshire Ripper murders. This may be completely unsubstantiated, but it reinforces the sheer paranoia in the towns of the West Riding during the Sutcliffe reign of terror, and it plays its part in an account of criminal history.

One definite piece of criminal social history of the town which is indicative of the problems caused by the explosive mix of poverty, cheap labour and factional oppositions can be seen in the story of how one markedly wild part of the area was brought within the law: this was Illingworth, Ovenden, a wild and lawless suburb in years gone by. In 1823 the situation regarding burglary and robbery was so extreme there that a jail was built. There were also village stocks, but the jail was a formidable and dour place. People incarcerated here were most likely about to be transported or whipped; but crime had been so terrible that harsh measures were needed. For instance, a gang actually came to use the jail building to stash a hoard, after an attack on a mill to steal silk. They took slates from the roof and put quantities of their silk there for safe keeping until it was needed. The jail was in operation until 1860.

The account of Illingworth jail makes a suitable prelude to the cases recounted in this book: many of the murders, suicides and assaults are related to the stresses and strains of keeping the wolf of starvation from the door in a tough era of extreme social change. (see chapter 9)

The research needed to excavate the narratives from the past has meant a reliance on the writers who have previously told the tales of local crimes, and the most helpful writers have been the *Evening Courier* writers in the newspaper and on their web site, and also those earlier writers who contributed to the almanacs up to the nineteen fifties. I have to thank these people.

I am also indebted to several people who have helped with this research, notably Kate Walker, who gave me first-hand information about crimes in the recent period; staff at the

Halifax Central Library, the writer Pat Posner, John Hargreaves, Bernadette Priestley, Peter Gregory and to Brian Elliott, the Series Editor.

Special acknowledgements are due to Edward Riley, editor of the *Courier*, for permission to reproduce images from the *Halifax Today Flashback* section on the *Courier* website.

CHAPTER 1

The Elland Vendetta

The story of the feud between Sir John Elland and the Beaumonts has been told so many times that legend and historical verification merge. In *The Yorkshire Magazine* for 1874 a note on a piece called 'The Last of the Ellands' observes that 'The MS from which the following legend is transcribed appears to be temp. Charles II... but the matter appears to have been drawn from original, ancient and trustworthy records...' The narrative is set in the reign of Edward III and the origin of the feud is located at around the year 1310. In a history of the parish of Halifax published in 1789 the tale is told with overblown and hyperbolic style. Almost killing the dramatic interest.

Despite this rather doubtful and confused account of its origins, the bloody murders perpetrated by Sir John Elland provides the earliest 'foul deed' known in any detail for this book. The folkloric element of the story lies in the typically oral narrative motifs of the supposed three blood stains given to Elland and his descendants as a curse by one

REVENGE UPON REVENGE:

OR, AN

HISTORICAL NARRATIVE,

OF THE

Tragical Practices

OF

SIR JOHN ELAND, OF ELAND,

HIGH SHERIFF

OF THE COUNTY OF YORK:

Committed upon the Perfons of Sir ROBERT BEAUMONT, and his Alliances, in the Reign' of EDWARD the Third, King of ENGLAND, &c.

TOGETHER,

With an Account of the Revenge which ADAM, the Son of Sir ROBERT BEAUMONT and his Accomplices took upon the Perfons of Sir JOHN ELAND and his Pofterity, herein fully, and plainly, as well as impartially reprefented, for the Satisfaction of the inquifitive Part of the World.

THE

WHOLE BEING DIVIDED INTO THREE EQUAL PARTS.

HALIFAX: E. JACOB, PRINTER

1789.

Front page of Jacob's Revenge Upon Revenge, *with the classic account of the Elland Feud. (1789)* The author

Wilfred the Saxon, but the more convincing elements concern the workings of the lawless society of the England of the early fourteenth century, as the account of the feud begins in the setting of the conflict between the Crown and the Earl of Lancaster.

Sir John Elland of Elland, a violent and wayward personality, greedy for land and power, is the villain at the heart of the story; he had that total baronial power explained well by the writer of the 1870 version: 'At that time when West Yorkshire was continually exposed to the forays of the Scots, the enforcement of the law of the realm in so wild a region was a difficult matter, and the lords of the manors exercised in their own districts powers of life and death as extreme as does a Highland chief at this day...'

The core of the conflict is about the local balance of power: the other influential families of the area, the Lockwoods, Quarmbys and Beaumonts, were forces to be reckoned with, but Elland had married one of the daughters of Sir William Beaumont of Crossland, and other daughters had married into the other powerful local families, so that when the old man died, and Elland was left only 500 gold marks, he was not happy.

At this point, all the versions of the tale insist on the outrageously amoral and brutal action of Elland, in going with armed men to the houses of the three enemies, and beheading the fathers in front of their wives. But the legend takes over the history with the act of Elland not killing the son of Beaumont (a small child) and thus the second stage of the story allows for the vengeance: 'At that his little son, who was not bound, smote Sir John with all his puny strength, crying out that they should not beat his father...'

The murders are described as barbarous in the extreme. '... the three gentlemen were made to lay on the block one by one their heads, which were smitten off.' Elland is depicted as a thoroughly unprincipled rogue, with no scruples, who wanted wealth, status and total sway over life and death in his manor and even beyond. The 1789 narrative talks about Elland 'designing to quench which malice had kindled in his breast, chose this season as an opportunity most apt and fitted for his purpose...(his majesty engaged in foreign wars...)'

Young Beaumont grows up, and while Elland is out hunting with his men and the dogs, he is cornered by the three sons of the men he had killed nineteen years previously, and they cut him down. The supposed 'historical narrative' as it is called by the author of the 1789 version, provides a typical example of the development of popular history in a local and regional context. The normal literary structure of the 'fall of princes' often used as a tragic storyline (as in Shakespeare) is here put into the rhetorical style in the eighteenth century habit, and then, in the Victorian re-telling, there is an attempt at adding historical context and amplifying the nature and importance of the kinship relations, allegiance and so on.

Nevertheless, the Elland vendetta is a narrative of genuine literary interest, and serves to place the pre-Renaissance crime stories in a tradition of popular genres: that is, the writers who took the basic story and re-told it, were adding their own contemporary embellishments. But at the heart of this tale is a foul murder, done for nothing but financial gain, and Sir John Elland is surely a villain to equal either the protagonists of the

Brookfoot, Elland, the centre of much of the action in the feud. The author

melodrama, or the evil done by men of status in an age of anarchy.

The story lived on into more literature; a long narrative poem written by the Reverend John Watson in 1775 describes the trap laid for Sir John at Cromwell Bottom, and makes Brookfoot Hill the focus, a place described by one writer as 'Killer Hill'. Some lines from the poem run:

> Beneath Brookfoot a hill there is
> To Brighouse in the way.
> Forth they came to the top of this,
> There prying for their prey.
> From the lane end then Eland came,
> And spied these gentlemen,
> Sore wondered he who they could be,
> And val'd his bonnet then

CHAPTER 2

Sowerby Witchcraft

I t would seem to be obligatory, in any research into regional or local crime in England, to find a case of witchcraft, and Halifax is no exception to this. The problem with these cases is, of course, that there is an alleged murder, and some poor woman is identified as a witch who caused the death, but naturally there is little on record to provide any data in direct evidence.

But the record is there, for 1598, and it concerns Agnes Walker of Warley, who supposedly caused the death of a clothier called Richard Stanfeild, of Sowerby Bridge. Warley, perhaps famous locally as the place where the famous novelist of Yorkshire history, Phyllis Bentley, lived in recent times, supports Bentley's assertion that Halifax has indeed its

A view of Warley from above today. The author

'romantic' side. But the tale of Agnes Walker is anything but romantic, and in fact confirms the other, darker side of the topography of Halifax – a place where it has always been easy for small settlements to be locked into isolation by the nature of the geomorphology of the region.

Warley is a small plateau one meets after scaling the heights of Tuel Lane, coming up from Sowerby Bridge. By road, if you are travelling towards Lancashire, it offers a right turn into attractive walking country, heading gradually towards the more 'Bronte' imagery of the moors. So it is not difficult to imagine the isolation here in the late sixteenth century, when ignorance of medicine was as widespread and dangerous as ignorance of basic learning; poor Agnes Walker, a widow, was convicted of Stansfeild's death, against whom she was supposed to have applied 'the diabolical arts' of sorcery.

The victim is said to have languished from August 1598 to January 1599, and Agnes was alleged to have 'killed and slew' him. The Statute of 5 Elizabeth c.16 made this possible. According to one source, only six cases were known in England in the reign of Elizabeth I. It comes as no surprise that the usual terms were used against Agnes and others: acts such as 'conjuration…invocations of evil or wicked spirits.'

It may have been the case that Mr Stansfeild had any one of a number of illnesses of which we now know a great deal. Therefore, in this particular Halifax 'murder' we have to use the term somewhat cautiously and with a large amount of doubt and disbelief. The modern mind would probably see Agnes Walker as the murdered person, not Stansfeild. The details of the case will never be further known, but it has to be reiterated that the superstition human communities are subject to thrives more in such isolated places. Halifax has an abundance of those locations, and Warley, as with Heptonstall, is one of the notable ones. Warley is particularly hidden from view, well beneath the road across from King Cross, nestling in a very secluded valley.

CHAPTER 3

The Wade Feud
1593

The story of one of the bloodiest feuds in the social history of Calderdale took place in Elizabeth I's reign, and it was initially all about who could own and profit from the trees growing in Crawood, near Luddenden. The woods there yielded high quality timber, and offered a rich prize to the right kind of entrepreneur. But some unsavoury characters and a few desperate, intransigent men figure in this incredible antagonism.

Samuel Wade, a member of a well-heeled local family, definitely wanted to get his hands on the trees; he was so resolved to win them at any cost, that in the end it cost him his life. In the year 1593, Samuel Wade lived at a house called Quickstavers in Sowerby, and across the valley at a place called Roebucks is the other family home that is central to the story. At the beginning, before things become complicated and trapped in legal difficulties, the basic fact is that Wade bought Roebucks, adjacent property, and (fatefully) the troubled woodlands of Crawood.

Now, Wade's brother-in-law bought Roebucks; he was Michael Foxcroft, and their business deal was to the effect that Foxcroft had to pay Wade £250 on or before 24 November, 1593, and it had to be at Quickstavers. The odd, very contrary character of Samuel Wade for some reason wanted his money paid in English silver coins – and nothing else. This kind of currency was known in the vernacular as 'white money'. It should all have been most straightforward, but Michael came to the agreed venue with the right amount, but in the wrong format. He brought a mixture of coinage, the silver part totalling £244, but the rest of the sum being a mix of European money.

Wade was a headstrong, wayward type who easily took offence and was officious in the extreme. He was obviously also quarrelsome and irascible. He refused to take the foreign currency as part of the deal. Understandably, in a bad mood but keen to settle things, Foxcroft went to his father in Halifax to obtain the acceptable format of money, and he did so, returning with the £6 in English silver. At this point Wade was not only moody but openly disagreeable and paradoxically unwilling to accept. He insisted that first of all Foxcroft should meet him with the money at sunset, and then still declined the sum, moaning that the man had not kept his side of the bargain.

The only explanation, apart from sheer awkwardness, was that both men wanted a reason to hold onto possession of that land and the coveted timber. They cavilled and used any strategy they could to outplay each other. Wade was patently using the letter of the law (and the status of a gentleman's agreement) to keep the prize. But things escalated out of control now.

Wade gathered what amounts to a private army, and the whole affair takes on the status of a large-scale feud. He had around sixty men with him to confront the Foxcrofts. The description of his gang given in the record is that they were 'armed with swords, daggers, long piked staves, axes, saws, bills and other unlawful weapons..' It was all clearly going to turn very savage indeed. Foxcroft had settled in at Roebucks, though, and Wade's men arrived to plunder the trees and they spent five days cutting down the trees. The value was said to be £160 (an immense sum of money then) and the men 'riotously' carried off the wood. The feud ended as they usually do: in a murder. Michael Foxcroft killed Samuel Wade in the back room of a tavern. The aggressive and wilful gang leader had met his end much as modern Mafia heads do – surprised and murdered when least expecting it. Wade's determined and recalcitrant attitudes recall many fictional accounts of confrontations and resentments festering inside people with their will to hold on to whatever wealth and power they can.

CHAPTER 4

Gibbet Law

In terms of the popular image of Halifax, as evidenced in heritage and tourist literature, the most notorious and macabre has to be the gibbet. Gibbet Street is still on the map, and the early drawings and engravings of the machine of death are testimony to the barbarity of this method of execution. According to J Horsfall Turner, one of the most respected antiquarians in the historiography of Halifax, the gibbet had been in the township 'since the remotest times, certainly from the Conquest of 1066.'

Reference books usually trace the origins of the guillotine to the Persian civilisation BCE. Examples of the gibbet notion are available in Britain well before the French guillotine; another well publicised example is the 'Maiden' in Edinburgh museum. In Germany there was a similar machine, used throughout the Middle Ages, known as the Diele or the Hobel.

The Gibbet, as sketched in Yorkshire Notes and Queries *1876.*

THE HALIFAX GIBBET.

In some earlier historical works, the Halifax Gibbet is a generic term used to explain the mode of execution known as the Gibbet Law, applied to felons convicted of theft.

Certainly, there is a whole literature of the gibbet, such is the fascination with this subject in the popular imagination, as indeed with the guillotine itself. Turner refers to a list of another hundred places in Yorkshire which had a gibbet, but the Halifax version continued well after the others. The historian of Halifax, Edward Jacob, writing at the end of the eighteenth century, explains this: 'As Halifax, however, was a place of so much trade, this custom, which was found to be so highly beneficial to the manufacturers there, that they kept it up as long as they durst.' The last execution done by this blade was in 1650, on 30 April, when two men, Mitchell and Wilkinson were beheaded. In Turner's book, *Biographia Halifaxiensis* (1883) he lists the beheadings which took place between 1541 and 1650. The total is forty-nine, and the most were effected in the reign of Elizabeth I– twenty-five in that period.

The list gives very little information about the specific crimes, and the most we have is for 'Richard Sharpe, de North, John Learoyd, de North, beheaded the fifth day of March 1568 for a robbery done in Lancashire.' Otherwise, the list simply notes that people were 'headed' and tiny details are added only seldom, such as George Fairbanke, executed in 1611, *vulgo vocatus Skoggin* – popularly known as … in other words, we have a slight touch of the human story there, beneath the statistics.

There are some popular folktales associated with the Gibbet, such as the story that a woman driving her cart to market (executions were on market days) passed by the platform and a criminal's head bounced into her cart. One writer notes about this that 'It is as reasonable to think that the whole tale is a little *Yorkshire*, which I suppose you will understand enough…'

Perhaps the tale most often told is the belief that if a man about to be beheaded could jump out as he heard the pin being slid out, and if he could run down to the river and across it, even if the executioner caught him, he could not be brought back to be killed. A folk story often given is of a man who managed to run for it, and was followed into the river by the executioner, and that the criminal was supposed to have shouted for the bystanders to get his hat for him. Such dark humour is, of course, to be expected.

The Gibbet itself was not made of a wooden frame, but a structure of stone, with stone steps. A drawing done in the mid-Victorian period shows a horse pulling the rope attached to the blade, and a broad stone platform around the base of the gibbet frame, with a slanting board running several feet down from the head-rest. The images of executions confirm the nature of the execution as a form of public entertainment, as in the more famous Tyburn Tree in London.

Even today, there is a certain dark atmosphere to the place where the Gibbet stood; it is surely a desperate and resonant irony that one of the most recent murders covered here, that of Emily Pye in 1957, was close to that spot. The presence of that awful wooden frame and the square of stone is something that still asserts itself in the historical imagination when one contemplates the rituals of death that were sustained in Britain for so long; after all, capital punishment was not abolished for all offences other than treason, piracy, arson in the royal dockyards and murder until 1868, and the voyeuristic fascination with public executions did not only affect the mob. Thomas Hardy had a morbid interest in watching hangings and made use of this in his fiction. A similarly strong narrative interest undoubtedly surrounds the Halifax Gibbet, and in a sense, its shadow stretches over the other cases covered in this book.

In the early nineteenth century, it looked as though there was no trace of the gibbet left; the wooden frame was thought to have rotted many years before, and the blade was not in evidence. But workmen in June, 1839 were digging in a heap of rubble and they found a stone platform – the one on which executions took place. The common belief at the time was that in the 1770s it was possible to see the platform but it was gradually covered in dirt and brick.

The Halifax historian and biographer of the Brontes, Francis Leyland, was fairly sure he knew where the platform would be, so the workmen perhaps were half expecting the find. They must have seen something similar to the picture taken of the platform about a century after this find. The actual blade had been removed to Wakefield. At the time of the find, the gibbet had been very much a prominent piece of interest, as there had been a play produced in 1833 called *Dennis*, or the *Gibbet Laws of Halifax*, written by the local writer, Thomas Crossley, the Ovenden Bard. A report of the time states that a facsimile of the gibbet was used, so accurate knowledge of what it was really like must have been available.

Finally, there was another discovery to be made at the site where the platform had been excavated. This was when a Mr Bates ordered some foundations to be dug as a new warehouse was being planned near the platform; the workers found two skeletons, and these are thought to be the remains of the last two gibbet victims, killed in that last recorded date of 1650: John Williamson and Anthony Mitchell.

CHAPTER 5

The Civil War: Death in Confinement

The Royalist commander, Sir Francis Mackworth, must have faced open resentment and a great deal of sullen opposition as he rode his men into Halifax, one of the centres of Parliamentarian loyalty in the English Civil War. There had been skirmishings across Calderdale, and a siege of Heptonstall which was notably unsuccessful. The West Riding towns had supported the Roundheads, and Halifax men figured prominently in the cause led in the north by Sir Thomas Fairfax.

But in June, 1643, a force under Fairfax was soundly beaten at the battle of Adwalton Moor and after that, as leaders of the Royalists secured various towns, Mackworth in Halifax needed a secure house for detainees in his headquarters. He chose a place once called South Place, later called the Corner House. This was in existence as a residence until it became commercial property owned by Hanson and Sons, and then was finally demolished. He was not here long, and the place was not a prison for very long, but there was an unfortunate victim of the situation. Mackworth had to leave soon after as

The Corner House at Southgate, where the Arcade Royale later stood. This was a prison for leading Roundheads. The author

How the Gibbet platform looked in the early twentieth century.

Marston Moor had put paid to the Royalists presence in the north , and Mackworth, after only six months in the town, was ordered to head north and face the Scottish forces.

In Mackworth's time as commander in the town, using the Corner House, there was one notable fatality under the regime: an officer called Joseph Priestley, who came from a well-known Sowerby family whose home was in Goodgreave. There is a romantic element to Priestley's sad demise; he had escaped to Lancashire after defeat of the Yorkshire forces, but had later returned to visit his wife but was captured at Blackstone Edge.

In confinement at the Corner House, he languished and died, despite the fact that he had been able to have two or three rooms for use there and that some of the other prisoners had commented that Priestley had been 'hearty and cheerful'in his stay there. Whether or not his death was due to the unhealthy state of the Halifax sanitation and air, as claimed, he was gone within a few days and it seems that he was buried behind the font in Halifax parish church.

Poor Joseph Priestley had paid the ultimate price for that trip across the hills to see his wife.

CHAPTER 6

The Cragg Vale Coiners Kill the Exciseman

The Coiners of Cragg Vale, when they murdered the exciseman, William Dighton in 1769, raised the local issue to the level of a national response, as the government, which had previously been remiss in issuing enough coinage for the circulation, published a proclamation on 10 November, stating that there would be a pardon for any person who would turn King's evidence, and a reward of £100 was offered for information leading to the arrest of the murderer. It was the response to a long-planned deed which had not been well done, as the two perpetrators had several failures before they actually trapped and shot Dighton.

The story is one of intrigue, double-dealing and incompetence. The core of the crime was the fact that coining had become a lucrative business for the group of men around 'King' David Hartley. Foreign currency was legal tender and some merchants were issuing their own money or, like Robert Wilson of Sowerby Bridge, were engraving brass plates to be esteemed the value of one guinea. It was fiscal chaos and a free-for-all, leaving the door open to 'clipping' – that is, shaving off gold from the coin-edges to melt and re-fashion into new coins.

The coiners gave 22 shillings for a full guinea, then sheared off the edge before cutting a new edge on the coin. It appears that there was about forty pence worth of gold from a clipping, and the moidore would have a value of 27 shillings, so there was a decent profit to be made. The gang thrived for some time: David, together with his brother Isaac (called The Duke of York), were at the centre. But in 1767 the local businessmen had had enough and Dighton was called in to investigate. The only option open to David Hartley and the others was to have Dighton permanently removed from the scene. When Hartley

Colne country, from Hebden Bridge. The author

was arrested and imprisoned, being taken at the *Old Cock Inn* in Halifax, on the word of a turncoat, James Broadbent, Dighton's death was looking far more likely.

The men given the job, Thomas Spencer, Robert Thomas and Matthew Normanton, went twice to a field near Dighton's house on Bull Close, but each time he was away and they missed him, increasing the frustration of the men who contracted the killing. On the third attempt, Spencer did not go, but Thomas and Normanton finally confronted the victim,

The Old Cock *in Halifax, where Hartley was arrested.* The author

and even then it was almost bungled, as Thomas's weapon misfired, but Normanton shot Dighton dead with his shortened shotgun. They stole what they wanted from his pockets and escaped. They had been drinking heavily and were now in the right mood to see the job done.

Swires Road, near to where Dighton was shot. The author

They returned to Mytholmroyd. In fact, the members of the group lived in places difficult to access, and remote from the town. Normanton lived at Stannery End, Thomas at Calder banks on the far slopes of the Calder; Isaac Hartley was at a place called Elphaborough Hall. David was nearer, at Bell Hole. The murder had taken place at a site which is now quite near the Bull Green area of the town – now a quiet junction of Swires Road and Savile Street.

The inquest opened in Halifax, and the first suspect was the informer, Broadbent. He had not been to work that day, but had been with his father, just drinking. He explained that he had been travelling to York on the day of the killing. But now, with the reward too large and tempting, Broadbent shopped the others: this brought about the arrest of Thomas, Normanton and another man, Folds.

At this point in the story, the famous Lord Rockingham, former Prime Minister and with his base at Wentworth Woodhouse, comes on the scene, gathering the local gentry. Things moved quickly, and by 1770 at the Spring Assizes in York, around two dozen coiners were on trial and David

Hartley and James Oldfield were sentenced to death. The whole saga of the retributions and recriminations in the gang is typical of that particular kind of ephemeral brotherhood in extreme crime, usually leading to a set of relationships depending solely on money and immediate gratification; men turned against former partners. Even two years after the trial, some men were giving fresh evidence.

But the murder was savagely avenged: Thomas and Normanton were hanged in York and their bodies chained up on Beacon Hill, their arms supposedly made to point in the direction of the murder scene. Normanton had been bailed, and had actually attempted to escape into the woods at Spa Laith, but he was tracked down hidden in briars and it was mooted that he could be executed then and there, but he was taken away.

The centre of the whole episode, the murder of an important local official, reminds us that the geography is so crucially important in understanding the foul deeds committed in Calderdale: the towns up the valley – Mytholmroyd, Luddenden Foot, Hebden Bridge and Heptonstall – are indeed very hard to penetrate. To drive into parts of these now is definitely a 'first-gear slope' experience. How easy was it then, in the days before efficient local transport, when footpads and highwaymen were universal, to feel that if you were a gang of desperate men on these slopes, the law would never reach you.

'King' David Hartley and the killers in his outfit were totally wrong on that point, and went to meet the hangman, but their tale has echoed down the centuries as one of the significant Halifax narratives of heinous and desperate murder. After all, the murder itself had been of a decent man doing his official duty, and he had been shot outside his home, with his wife in bed and a servant coming out to look for him, after a long day of negotiations at Cottingley, helping to solve a dispute.

The Dighton murder had been close to town, among decent people, and done ruthlessly by men who put illegal earnings before honour and honesty. There was never going to be any mercy for them. Things had not changed much by the end of the century: a woman was hanged at Tyburn for coining in 1789, for instance.

CHAPTER 7

Murder Among the Fools
c.1760

In the years of the mid-eighteenth century, a colourful character called Johnny Worral used to be taunted and teased by the young women of Halifax, as they asked him to throw his hat in the air. He obliged, and gleefully threw and caught his hat for them. We tend to associate licensed fools with Shakespearean comedy, but Worral was indeed that, by profession almost. The real facts about him are not known for sure, but there was a dark side and a mystery to the man.

In an engraving of 1759 he is depicted as 'Johnny Worral, Halifax lunatic.' In fact, he was welcomed into the homes of the wealthy, and even went to Shibden Hall as a guest. He was known by everyone it seems, and his garish and bizarre dress sense was part of that appeal. When he was asked where he obtained these clothes, he said he was 'a cunning, sharp lad, else he could never get such.' The owner of Shibden at the time, James Lister, says in a letter that Worral had visited him and entertained them, 'taking part in some tomfoolery.' His status in society is of great interest, and it would seem logical to surmise that he was something similar to what would today be a mix of a guest speaker and a party entertainer.

A 1759 engraving of Johnny Worral.

But there is a complication too, in this tale. This is because another character on record, one Hal Pierson, may well have been Worral in fact. Pierson was supposed to be employed by Sir George Armytage as a fool at Kirklees Hall, but an old portrait which is supposed to be Hal is identical to that of Worral. Whatever the actual facts, Hal or Worral was said to have been mercilessly teased and baited by a man called Robbie, who was a carpenter, and one day the worm turned, as the madman claimed to have done a 'bonny trick' on the workman, saying that he had hidden the man's head under a pile of wood shavings, and that 'when he wakes he'll be troubled to find it...' The truth was that the supposed friendly lunatic had indeed decapitated the unfortunate man.

Hal/Worral was tried at York but was deemed insane and was allowed to be taken back to be in the care of Armytage. He died aged thirty, and the description of him then is that he was 'white haired and feeble.'

CHAPTER 8

The One-Pound Note Murder
1817

Another murder story from Calderdale, this time from a site near Hebden Bridge, ended in two culprits trying strenuously to put the blame for the murder of old Samuel Sutcliffe of Hawden Hole squarely on the shoulders of the other. The double-dealing did them no good. Both John Greenwood (known as Jon o't' Bogg Eggs) and his accomplice, Michael Pickles (nick-name Old Mike) did not keep them from the noose.

The story began with yet another local issue relating to currency. It was the habit of local tradesmen to produce their own bank notes, and these were used and respected as widely

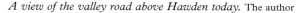

A view of the valley road above Hawden today. The author

as the normal government-issue notes. One of these companies issuing their own notes was that of Sutcliffe of a place called The Lee. A particular note for one pound would prove to be decisive in finding the murderers, Mike and Greenwood.

The killing took place on 7 February 1817. The victim was one Samuel Sutcliffe of Hawden Hole, and he had been strangled and robbed. Sutcliffe also had a nick-name (as everyone seems to have done) and this was 'Sammy o' Katty's.' He was a bachelor of eighty years, a maker of worsted pieces. On Saturdays he and his nephew often went to Halifax market, and he was a hale and hearty man for his age, strongly independent, and with a nest-egg from his life of hard work and application to his skills.

Hawden Hall, now modernised, is overlooked by a yew-tree and is indeed a quiet spot with a certain atmosphere. In 1817, the dwelling was single-storey and had another place, that of William Greenwood, adjoining. Clearly, he was vulnerable: old and quite well off, living in a place which was generally quiet and closed in. Older photos show a barn, and this has now gone too, so there is more of a sense of open ground.

Mike Pickles, 'Old Mike', lived at Northwell near Heptonstall. He was a weaver there, but also did outdoor work such as dry-stone walling and notably, he did 'weiring' – brickwork near rivers and streams to protect the land nearby. He was markedly strong and would show off the power of his left hand, crushing objects with great force.

His partner in crime, John Greenwood, was a close friend and they had married sisters. They planned what was to be a robbery only, sitting up late and waiting until midnight for the assault on the old man. The main narrative, told by WS Baring-Gould, insists that John was less sanguine about the crime than Old Mike. But they went into Sutcliffe's house and Old Mike found a box in which Sutcliffe kept his papers and other valuables. The old man awoke, and to shut him up, Old Mike strangled him. The murderers took cotton pieces, shirt and shoes.

This is where the pound-note enters the tale. In the oak box there were a guinea note and some Bank of England notes.

The fastness of Hebden Bridge, from the Lancashire Road, showing the impenetrable nature of the place in Victorian times. The author

Here, the crucial fact is that one of the notes was one of the local unsigned notes, this one from Mytholmroyd Mill. The note then began its circulation around the community, going from hand to hand until one Mrs Wadsworth tried to use it to buy some supplies and the shopkeeper did not accept it, as of course, it was not signed. The note had originally being given to Thomas Greenwood, who could not read, and did not know which note he had passed on to Mrs Wadsworth. When Greenwood learned about the unsigned note, he knew that it was one which had gone to the dead man, and that it was missing – and in the murderer's hands.

Of course, suspicion fell on old Sutcliffe, but it soon shifted in the direction of the two actual culprits; the evidence against them was now forming and becoming absolute confirmation of their guilt. One story is that Old Mike was troubled and could not eat after doing the deed, and that he came across a woman in Northwell Lane on the Friday morning. When he asked her if she knew that 'Old Sammy' had been murdered, she is reputed to have said, 'If he is, it's thee that's done it!'

The melancholy yew-tree is there, and there is little to hint at the once notorious case: the trial and the full story were widely reported at the time, even to the point of hawkers in Leeds selling long word-for word accounts of the statements made, and Baring-Gould, who first told the story in great detail in print, actually says that he was given information taken from the *Hebden Bridge Chronicle* of 1856, and that 'the papers of the compiler have been kindly sent to the author.' This means that the Hawden Hole case is the one murder of the nineteenth century in this area of which almost every detail is known and clearly recorded. The long, deep-cut valley, seen to advantage from the bridge on the Burnley road, is very difficult to access.

Once again, the case exemplifies the tendency of most victims of murder to be known by their killers, and for the basis of the crime to be rooted in a narrow, defined locality, in which there is always temptation for the have-nots, based on knowledge of the 'haves' – in this case, the few possessions of an old and frail, hard-working man were the cause of the killing.

CHAPTER 9

The Gaol Problems
1820s

alifax was indeed a wild and dangerous place in many of its darker areas in the early nineteenth century. What is now the Woolshops, by the Piece Hall, was one such place, and the oldest timber building in the town, now a café, shows this history, being set in one of the most perilous parts of the town, often changing ownership. Looking at it today, on the side of the square just before the walker reaches the markets, it is easy to imagine the wildness around that vestige of a more violent time.

Generally in Britain in the early decades of the nineteenth century, there was much discussion of the prison problems;

Illingworth Gaol as it was in 1973. The stocks are behind railings on the left.
Evening Courier

The oldest timber building surviving in Halifax, once in the heart of the dangerous Woolshops area. The author

the debates were raging about more enlightened forms of imprisonment than the usual methods. After all, this was the time when prison hulks were moored on the Thames, and in which prisoners in most places were forbidden to mix with others, even being isolated at times of prayer in the chapels.

But Halifax had a problem with crime so severe that it had no time for philosophic sentiment or prolonged political discussion. In particular, the area of Illingworth and Ovenden was so rife with crime that things were going too far. Even the vicarage was robbed, and an iron safe taken from the church.

In 1823 a gaol was built in Illingworth to provide a quick solution to this. It was built on the corner of Keighley road, by the parish church. It had four cells, well barred, and served as a temporary lock-up as felons were in transit to official courts for trial. On their way to severe punishment (most commonly transportation), they actually had bedding provided in Illingworth: very unusual at that time, when people were still trying to absorb some of John Howard's reforms of prisons while houses of correction were yet forbidding places with cruel regimes.

There was an inscription over the door of the gaol: 'Know Thyself' and one wonders whether this had any effect on the villains (or whether many could read the words). The move

In 1969 these children visited the long disused Illingworth Gaol. Evening Courier

seemed to have some effect, eventually, as it was no longer used from the date 1860, being sold to the co-operative society, and was then used as a store-room. Now it has another life as a private garage.

Surely the most remarkable story associated with the gaol is the tale that a bunch of thieves broke into nearby factories to steal silk (a successful new industry in Ovenden around 1830). But they then headed for the gaol; they stashed their booty under the slates from the prison roof, to come back for later.

There may have been debates in parliament and attempts to reform some of the more barbaric elements in the penal code, but in Halifax, they had a problem and they sorted it – and the prisoners had a reasonably good few nights there, comparatively well cared for.

CHAPTER 10

Robbery and Strangling
on the Road
1839

This story from one of the most tumultuous and rough decades in the history of Britain, being the years of the rise of Chartism, illustrates the sheer desperation and opportunism of a gang of robbers. The pursuit of the gang went from Stump Cross, across to Burnley, and then even to Dublin, before the case was resolved. It also highlights the perilous nature of travel at that time.

A scan of the *Leeds Mercury* for these years indicates the widespread problem of what we might now call mugging, but then was undoubtedly a frightening mixture of hard criminal gangs or even the continuation of the 'highway robbery' so prevalent in the last years of the previous century. In this case of the two businessmen from Halifax, Robert Crossley and Thomas Cockcroft, the narrative even throws light on other aspects of the social history of crime in northern England, and indeed generally, as the local constable and the Dublin officers of the law come out of the tale with a high degree of professionalism and dedication.

It all began when the two businessmen had to travel from Halifax to Doncaster. Cockcroft was a wool merchant and needed to travel to the Doncaster wool market. They made the arduous journey, did their business transactions, and then set off for home in Mr Cockcroft's trap. As they left around four in the afternoon, it was dark when they neared home. They must have later wished that they had broken their journey at Wakefield, where Crossley had family connections; but they pressed on as the weather was clement.

The journey has a feel of absolute terror about it, for they approached Lower Brear and met a man called Downs, who passed by and appeared to be no danger. But they were still on the road and it was near midnight. At that point a group of five men ranged across the road in front of them, threatening some harm and the boldest, a thug called Daunt Rushworth (real name Jonathan) grabbed the horse. Cockcroft was quick-thinking and dashed into a nearby field, throwing his purse into the dark there.

A sustained fight followed this, extremely violent. Rushworth was cracked across the face with Crossley's horse-whip; then he was overpowered and in the grip of several men. One of the most brutal, one Barber, threatened him and tried to throttle him, as others robbed his person. Crossley must have been physically strong and resolute, as he fought back, and was jammed against a wall by several men, and Barber is reputed to have said, 'Tha shall tell no tales about me...'

The attack was frustrated in many ways: they could not recover the money from the field, there was little found in the trap, and even Crossley's hat was of no use to Barber, as it had the owner's name sewn in it. It was sheer frustration that led Barber to return to his victim, with the intention of kicking him to death but his accomplices restrained him. Crossley had no better fortune: another robber called Dawson, came at him with a knife, but eventually the gang fled. The two victims managed to travel onwards in the trap.

After the attack the tale becomes one of a long, determined and tough pursuit of the desperadoes, through Lancashire and to Ireland. The Halifax constable, Fraser, and a detective, traced the gang to Burnley races, and here the account of the Rushworth gang becomes something close to the Scarlet Pimpernel adventures, for even when shackled by the law at Burnley, the villains appealed to the mob, pretending they were apprehended Chartists: 'Brother Chartists, will you see us sacrificed?' Dawson said. The nasty group of wrong-doers had been up to more mischief in Burnley, and only Rushworth was apprehended, as the others went to Dublin. Rushworth was identified by Crossley, who is supposed to have been lenient, as the man could have taken his life that night on the road. He went to the York Assizes for trial.

Meanwhile, in Dublin, police had taken hold of the thugs, and Fraser, who had followed, after some difficulties in proving who he was, had them brought back to Yorkshire. At

Gaol Lane today. Many a criminal passed this way, under arrest. The author

the *New Inn* on Blackstone Edge, the Halifax and Dublin officers had the coach-horses changed. Even at this point, two men shackled together made a run for it across the fields, and were pursued by Fraser and a civilian, the criminals making good ground across a stream, but they were tracked down.

In town, in Gaol Lane, the culprits were taken through Upper George Yard and tried by John Waterhouse at a hearing

Upper George Yard, where the highwaymen were taken in 1839. The author

in the gaol rather than at the court-house (at Ward's End), and it seems that the prisoners absolutely refused to move out of the gaol. But the following March they were tried in York where life was commuted to fifteen years' hard labour. So ended one of the most exciting stories of violent crime and determined pursuit in the history of Calderdale.

CHAPTER 11

Saddleworth Patricide
1840

This murderer was a young man who terrorised his village and neighbours, and set about his own mother with a knife. So fearful was she of her own wild son that she left to live with relatives in America. The whole neighbourhood must have been relieved when the twenty-three-year-old man was finally punished, saying prayers with his eyes closed before being hanged in front of a crowd of more than a thousand.

Much of the literature and myth of the wild Pennine moors concerns a landscape in which the human habitation has often, as is the case with many lonely and marginal communities, been subject to rare and singular conditions. Whether this explains the tragic crime of patricide is doubtful, but Emily Bronte, for instance, depicts in the Earnshaws a family not far removed from the amorality bound up in the sad story of James Bardsley, who was executed for murdering his father 'at the new drop behind the Castle, York' in this year.

A distant view of wild Saddleworth, where numerous crimes of a brutal nature are on record, including the sad story of James Bardsley. The author

The story of his last hours is indeed a miserable one: he would not speak, and was attended by a priest who clearly tried to comfort him, and to elicit some kind of explanation or perhaps a catharsis. But Bardsley had 'throughout his condemnation maintained a perfect silence' according to the *Halifax Guardian* report.

Bardsley's father John had worked for a Mr Peter Sevile at Lees on the Yorkshire-Lancashire border and had a good local reputation as an upright citizen. He must have been profoundly ashamed of his lawless son, and it seems that there may well have been a serious mental illness at the core of Bardsley's being; but this happened in 1840, well before such things were known or discussed.

On Sunday, 1 November of that year, John Bardsley was reading his Bible, in the company of his daughter and another child who was visiting, when his son came in and helped himself to some bread and cheese. His father's remonstrance must have been the last straw after events earlier in the day, because he 'snapped', lost control and drew a knife. He set about his father with this and wounded him severely in the face and the body. The sister had run from the house as soon as her brother had arrived; and now a crowd of people arrived seeing the horrible sight of the son bending over the body of his father, lying on the floor in a pool of blood.

One of the most striking aspects of the story is that when Bardsley was taken away, in temporary custody until the law arrived, it was to a public house, and here he had drinks and food, tucking in with enthusiasm, the blood of his father staining his hands and arms. The neighbours were aghast at this, obviously unable to comprehend the man's indifference to what he had done.

James Bardsley left this world at York, from the drop, and the witness writing the report noted that although he was a slight man, the death was quick – unlike the agonising slaughter he had perpetrated on his own good father. It has to be said there are more intriguing questions unanswered in the tale, than given in the reports. It is a story with perhaps a shadowy parallel tale, the one involving where and when and how Bardsley 'went wrong' and what plans if any were made to cope with him after his mother's escape from his reign of terror.

CHAPTER 12

Cruelty to a Collier Boy
1843

The apprenticeship indenture system, under which the boys in training were legally bound, potentially almost as slaves, to their masters, was clearly open to terrible abuse in the Victorian era. This tale is in some ways the most truly pathetic in the accounts of cruelty and ill-doing in the Halifax area.

It concerns two people with the same surname, but not apparently related, and it occurred in Elland. The dominant image – and it haunts the imagination of anyone reading this story today – is of a drunken master drifting from public house to public house, leaving a boy supposedly in his care to starve near to death.

Joseph Whiteley was a collier from Elland, and James Whiteley the boy, and the case of cruelty had been previously examined under the Children's Employment Commission, but in 1843 the case was brought again, by the boy, with a Mr Holdroyde acting for an Overseer of the parish, Mr Dodgson, to try to attain some reparation for the boy, who had been treated worse than an animal.

James, after seven years in the employment of Whiteley, could tolerate the abuse no more and ran away, and when he was traced and brought before the magistrates, but so extreme was the offence of the master, and the evidence so apparent, that it was dismissed. The main offence was actual physical cruelty. Whiteley had taken his belt to the boy and whipped him, the buckle digging into his flesh. Under an act of George III, c57, s 11, there were potentially at least, firm actions to be taken against the master, but this was not effected.

After Whiteley was ordered to change his attitudes and behaviour and care for the boy in the way accepted in accordance with the apprenticeship system, he left the court and was seen by a constable later in the day consorting with known prostitutes as the boy was left outside; then he moved along to another drinking-house.

Throughout the recent period after the first hearing, the boy had been kicked, bruised deeply, and it was reported that he had been so badly used on a particular day that the overseers of the workhouse insisted that he be seen by a physician. Then defence merely offered something 'in extenuation', implying a payment to a charity or most probably to the workhouse in question. But the fact is that at *The Lamb* public house, Whiteley had acted in a way which confirmed his intention to continue abusing the unfortunate young man.

Through our eyes, the outcome seems bland indeed. The malefactor was fined £10 – a very large sum then, but a prison sentence would seem just to us. However, the most telling event of the whole case was the response of the justice, the presiding magistrate, Mr Pollard, who reportedly gave a long speech, emotional and impassioned, lamenting that under the law he could not act in any way that would have seemed a just punishment for such savagery.

The overseers and guardians would find young Whitely a new position: so at least he would be free from the monster who had almost killed him. The medical evidence stated that the boy, at the worst stage, 'had an eruption at various parts of his body... caused by the lad not being well fed.' All the lawyers and officials expressed their revulsion at the extremity of the case, and it is clear that there was a general feeling of frustration at not being able to do for the boy what should have been done.

It is plain to see that the area of Elland at that time was a tough and wild place: the report makes a special mention of this reputation, noting that ' this case of unexampled barbarity came from Elland, a neighbourhood which had already figured in the report of the Commission...' The note of criticism is very strong.

This kind of cruelty, leading to a condition of near-death for a boy in his care, is indeed one of the cruellest acts found in this social history, and it is easy to be reminded of the similar criminal narratives widespread in the period when employment acts were unreformed, and such types of heartless exploitation could be done with little legal redress.

CHAPTER 13

Murder at Mount Tabor
1843

igh above Luddenden, close to Moor End, lies the village of Mount Tabor, and in the lonely, hard-working days of the weavers' cottages at the height of the domestic industry, the cruelty of a father eventually led to another case of patricide. It would be too simple to look at such facts, arising partly from the father's desire for money at the cost of human closeness and true family values. But that would leave too much out.

For this is a story of that specific type of revenge which comes from a moral sense of innate justice: in fact a crime of passion, in a sense. The son of John Dobson, Joe, shot his father dead after years of cruelty and abuse. The external, bare facts make it a pre-meditated crime, and so murder, not manslaughter, but there is much more complexity than this in the sorry tale.

It began with the hard, uncompromising widower, John Dobson, working long hours together in a cottage owned by Joseph Birtwhistle. The writer of the main retrospective account of the killing, writing in 1899, wants to put some of the blame for the wife's death at John's door, but that is part of the unknown 'backstory' of this murder. The fact is that the father treated the son extremely harshly, feeding him only on water porridge, to save money, but working him long and hard. Even when, for a long period, Joe was the sole worker, the father still treated him harshly.

Joe was earning eighteen shillings a week then, a reasonably substantial sum, but he had to live with a father who constantly goaded and annoyed him. One day, Joe tried to run out and buy himself some proper food. But the old man followed him, attacked him with a rolling pin, and finally locked him up in one of the rooms of the house. It was clearly the last straw: Joe ran away to find work in Wakefield, and in his absence, neighbours, who had often heard cries of pain as the boy was bullied, thought there had been some foul play.

The amazing thing about the story is that Joe later sent for his father to join him in Wakefield, now that decent work had been found for both of them. The relationship was volatile from the start, and nothing ever went smoothly: Joe joined the army, and even then he was subject to the persuasion of his father, who urged him to desert, and when he did so, he gave his father a source of real threat amounting to blackmail should there be a problem later.

The crux of the tale is Joe's marriage. When he married and brought his new wife to live with his father after trying to exist by themselves in a few places. This was a recipe for disaster. John Dobson hated the girl. Joe and his wife had two children by this time, and there were pressures in the home, in every sense. The father and daughter-in-law constantly quarrelled, and these rows became more and more violent. Eventually, in July, 1843, Dobson, armed with a razor, threatened her life. There was a furore, and Constable Birtwhistle placated things, or so he thought (Joe being away at the time).

When Joe returned and learned what had happened, naturally he was furious and they had a major confrontation. Joe threatened that he would shoot his father, so much did he hate him. The constable managed to attempt a settling of the situation, but no-one had any idea that Joe would set out and find a gun, borrowed from Harry Thomas at Brownhirst. He had to be determined to do the deed, as he had to go further, somewhere else, to find shot, caps and powder. Finally, he decided on a gun that was in the home of one John Lassey, and then he was ready to do the deed.

Joe walked home and found not his father there, but a neighbour, Jim Snowden, who of course tried to calm Joe. But his father arrived and immediately provoked him, goading him to shoot. The first attempt failed, and Jim Snowden ran out for help. The second shot hit home and the father went down dead, with the family looking on.

Joe ran off in a panic and the chase was on. The first pursuit failed and he made his escape; then he was seen in a public house (*The Duke* at Clarke Bridge). But he eluded the law. It wasn't until he surfaced at Huddersfield, recognised by someone called Speight who had known him since childhood. He was arrested and carried off.

At York, before the death sentence was passed, Joe made a powerful speech in defence of his actions, pleading for some understanding of his mental condition after so many years of tyranny and abuse. The 1899 memoirist says, 'I once had a mother, three brothers and a sister, and all of 'em came to death from the punishment he has given them...' Maybe today, with a good lawyer, there would have been a different outcome.

But Joe Dobson, ready to face his maker, stepped towards the drop at York on 30 January. The hangman is reputed to have said, 'Goodbye and God bless you Dobson' to which Joe responded:

'I am in His arms now.' The reader of this tragic tale cannot help wondering if this was a blessed release the poor man had longed for over those harsh, tormented years.

CHAPTER 14

Slaughter in the *Guardian* Offices
1858

Halifax was notable for many trades by the early nineteenth century, and one of the most prominent ones was undoubtedly printing. Trade directories for the first years of Victoria's reign list around a hundred printers. It was also a good place to learn the craft of journalism. There had been a newspaper, financed by Lord Savile, in the eighteenth century, but by the early nineteenth century, the *Halifax Guardian* had become most successful. But one horrendous story in the annals of that estimable journal concerns the truly awful murder committed by a senior apprentice, William Blackburn Dawson.

The killing happened in 1858, and Dawson is most certainly an example of what modern criminology understands in the category of the tortured loner, the killer with a whole bundle of inner stresses and strains which are latent, powerful and in this case, most deadly.

It was the 8 May and the young men working in the *Guardian* offices in George Street were busy in the large jobbing department. This was a room on the first floor, behind the adjoining room used by the various editors and reporters. There were five young men working regularly together in this room: one of them was James Edward Jacobs, a descendant of the local historian Edward Jacobs whose *History of Halifax* provides us with the most dramatic account of the Elland revenge. Poor James had no idea what that fateful day held in store for him as he was working setting up a case, and apparently feeling quite ill.

The other young workers were Samuel Hyslop, Samuel Harris and Fred Foster, all getting on with their work as Dawson exercised with some dumb bells. The day was probably quite routine: it seems like the kind of recreation Dawson did with a firm sense of routine and discipline, but

The entrance of the Courier *office today. The author*

through modern eyes, it does smack of the 'life' prison environment in popular culture: all that pent-up energy in a man who was sublimating a dangerous package of destructive feelings, ready to implode in him.

Now, Dawson was, according to the report written in 1898, a quiet young man who was 'melancholy and taciturn'. He was suffering from hallucinations and 'his life had been one horrid nightmare' Even more suggestive of some infamous twentieth century crimes is the note that 'he had considerably overgrown his strength.' To compound the situation, he also was under the delusion that he had some nasty wasting disease which was slowly draining him of life, and the medical advice that it was 'all in his mind' had been patently ignored.

Dawson was going through the exercise routine just after the lunch hour period, and as Jacobs was feeling ill, he asked Dawson (on good terms with him generally) to bring him some snuff from another room. He brought this for his workmate, and calmly said so, before lifting the dumb-bells again. But then came some cataclysmic release of some immense inner pain and confusion in him.

The men reported hearing a deeply agonised and terrifying scream coming from Dawson, just seconds before he slammed a dumb-bell sphere smack onto the head of poor Jacobs in front of him, bending over the case. Looking up, the other men saw Dawson standing over Jacobs, about to crash the huge weight down on his victim again. They all tried to dash at him to restrain him, but he threw the things at them, stained as they were with blood and hair from poor young Jacobs. He was so crazed and strong that he drove them out of the room and fastened himself in with a rod across the door.

Dawson then grabbed a thick iron bar from a

A view of the Courier *office showing the upper rooms.* The author

screw-press and set about attacking Jacobs once more. All this time, he was howling like a wild beast in his fury. The other young men tried to ram the door to gain access, but made no progress. Now a woolstapler outside, Bates, and another worker called Tiffany, came to help and the latter kicked the door open. As the crowd rushed in, they were met by Dawson, howling and wielding an iron press-pin which weighed twenty-one pounds and was over five feet long. There was a sustained and furious struggle with the madman (as that is what he was now) and he made a rush to escape.

A man called Rothwell had the courage to take him on, and the penalty for tackling Dawson was that he was held in a vice-like grip. Then a man named Bates came to help, and a chance was created for the general group to seize and overpower the furious Dawson. The killer was now covered in blood and fragments of Jacobs' brains. The writer in 1898 remarks that Dawson is supposed to have said, 'I've just missed it in one point, I ought to have chopped Jacobs' head off, and thrown it out of the window...'

The final detail in this foul record of atrocity is that when they eventually checked on Jacobs' body, they found that his head and face had been chopped and sliced by a hatchet. It appears that this is a case of a man whose mind 'snapped' but it is hard to put it down to such modern concepts as 'work-place stress' and schizophrenia seems a more likely explanation.

At the inquest, the definition of what had gone on was 'wilful murder' yet when the doctor, giving evidence, had mentioned the illness which Dawson fancied had him in its grip, he again gave out the horrific howl of pain that he had done on the day of the murder. Even in court, he tried a similar move to attack and it took six men to restrain him.

Dawson died in the lunatic asylum to which he was committed after leaving York Castle. It was noted that he had become calm and quiet, speaking with sanity and normality about his 'friend' poor Jacobs. When asked why he had done such an outrageous act, he had no answer. His decline presents to the modern reader a fascinating mixture of sympathy and disgust: in the end, it is yet another tale of crime in which a mental condition was not recognised then, and a killing was just that, and no more.

CHAPTER 15

Found Under a Carpet
1859

A certain William Hall of Soyland presents us with a truly mysterious death; the record of his death indicates a high level of probability that there was foul play somewhere, but in 1859 the inquest found that he had been found dead in his house 'with marks of strangulation' but there was insufficient evidence to prove wilful murder.

The man was found lying under a carpet with a cord tight around his neck. He was a widower of 64, a clothier who went to Huddersfield market, and indeed his body was found at the close of market day. Since his wife's death just five months before, it had been observed that he drew his curtains close and kept himself to himself, so that when the police entered his home (through a window) they went downstairs to his private room and found the body.

The marks made by the cord did suggest a knot was made, so that a consideration of suicide was followed, but there had been a burglary also a short time before, so things were becoming complicated. Mr Roberts did a medical report and said that plenty of circumstances made suicide almost impossible as a conclusion regarding the death. But even more confusion and doubt enter the case when one considers the statement made by his son, Joseph, who lived nearby. He stated that various people had owed his father money, including sums of £20 and £5 – a large amount then.

Joseph also said that his father had reported being robbed to him not long before this fateful night. We seem to have a story which may be read in two very different ways: first, there is the possibility of the man suffering from severe depression and internalising his grief after his wife's death, thus being isolated and perhaps open to thoughts of suicide. Second, that he was indeed robbed and murdered, the carpet being placed over his body either as an insult or as some kind of ironical comment on the man's business. The suicide seems highly unlikely.

That leaves us with a probable scenario in which the lonely man was robbed and attacked, maybe by one of his debtors, who had a rankling hatred of the old man, and wanted to not only kill him and thus erase the debt, but also suggest something about the man's nature as a businessman. If the latter is the case, then it doesn't entirely hold water, as the son would have still been able to claim the debt.

As Holmes would have said, we are only left with the improbable as the most likely: that he was killed by an insane intruder or by a desperate one, who was perhaps even known to the victim. Whatever the truth (and we shall never know) the carpet was a twisted piece of humour.

CHAPTER 16

A Pub Brawl Killing
1865

Tom Yeadon, a labourer living in Mill Lane, would never have imagined that a night out drinking a few pints in his local would end in his death. Yeadon, aged thirty five and normally of a quiet disposition, went to spend some time at the *Royal Hotel* and what happened next was typical of thousands of arguments, beginning in some taunting and teasing, and then escalating into a confrontation. It could have been partly the time of year – just after Christmas – and people still full of drink. But it was nasty and violent in the extreme.

The man who took exception to Tom Yeadon was Joe Womersley. A witness, called Garfitt, saw the beginning of the fight – something personal taken as a dire insult, and then, within seconds, Womersley was confronting Yeadon, stripped off ready to have a scrap in earnest, and he did so, taking hold of Yeadon, slamming him down hard onto a pub table, and then holding him in a vice-like grip. There were plenty of people in the tap-room at the time, and a man called Kenworthy bravely parted them.

The Old Town Hall, where Womersley was seen, usually wanting a fight.
The author

Garfitt says that Womersley struck Yeadon on the head before they were forced apart, and then that both men returned to their own seats. He said that he left the *Royal* at around ten o'clock, and at that point things appeared to be relatively calm, and he stated in court that he wasn't sure of what damage had actually been done. One thing was for sure: both men had been considerably drunk at the time, and the provocation seems to have referred to the sexual prowess of Mr Womersley.

But the apparent calm was not a resolution; Yeadon made his way home and then began complaining of a pain in his chest. He gradually worsened and the day after he was delirious and violent. The doctor, a Mr Farrar of Brighouse, was called in, but Yeadon died on 31 December. There was uncertainty about this case, as there was no clear idea given of the exact nature and force of the blow given by Womersley on Yeadon. Where there is doubt, there is almost certainly a verdict of accident death, but the testimonies indicate that Womersley was very aggressive and applied a great deal of force when he first applied a head-lock and then struck the unfortunate Tom Yeadon.

The full truth will never be known, but in the end, it is a case of a few rash words leading to a violent death – a killing or 'natural causes'. Whatever the ultimate cause of death, having one's head held in a savage grip and being pummelled around the brain would not help to preserve good health.

Drink as a factor causing violent crime was a huge problem at this time. James Burnley, a Bradford journalist, visited the West Riding Prison in 1880 and gave this staggering statistic:

'... during the last seven years, the committals for drunkenness have been more than doubled. In 1867 there were 1186 persons imprisoned for this vice...'

Joe Womersley was lucky not have joined the desolate men in the white-washed cells of Wakefield for this rash act. His attack seems to have been a drunken rage.

CHAPTER 17

Attacked for Name-Calling
1865

The first report of this very nasty and brutal crime was reported as an 'Irish outrage' and this obviously relates to recurrent problems in a particular community of poor labouring people. It happened in winter, and involved a group of people at odds over being abused in the street, and ended with a terrible assault on a woman in her own home.

Edward Welsh and Pat Calligan, two manual workers, were charged with assaulting Margaret May in January of this year. The victim could not speak English properly and her daughter spoke for her. The story is that late one night, Welsh had called May names, shouting in the street, replying to names she had supposedly screamed at him. He called her 'whore, bitch and antichrist.' May had referred to him as an 'old gun-stealer.' The train of violence began when Welsh came to her and hit her hard on the head with a stick.

He had come to her door and railed at her, and after being struck, she went inside to fetch her shawl, but as she came back, Welsh hit her on the breast with a poker. He went for her, swearing that he would kill her. A young man grabbed hold of him, but then Calligan came to try to join in and the door was slammed in his face. There had been a noisy and general disturbance now for some time, and a James Broader of Shay Lane saw much of this. He said that he heard Welsh say that he would 'have a bit of your limbs' at one point.

Margaret May was house-bound for a long period between the assault and the trial, severely injured. There had been months of name-calling and a generally uneasy situation in the street. She had often called him a mischief and a 'monkey'. But others began to take sides at the trial. Bridget, May's daughter, was there all the time of the attack, but her

The Market buildings, where a street fight involving Irish immigrants broke out in 1865. The author

statement was contradicted by Nancy Gannon, who said that there was no violence until Welsh was provoked. It is clear that Gannon was projected as an upright citizen when hauled in to testify, as she sated that she was 'a mother of nine children… and have never been called to a place like this before.'

It seems incredible through modern eyes that the men were given fines of three pounds or six weeks in gaol. The victim had actually given a deposition to an official, as it was believed that she would die. It was patently very close to being a

One of the alleys between Dean Clough and Shroggs Road and Corporation Road, where several attacks are recorded from mid-Victorian years. The author

murder, and all over a verbal interplay of abuse meeting further abuse. But there had been wider problems perceived within the Irish community at this time. Two weeks after this, a man was almost beaten to death in an alley by *The Shears* public house and kicked repeatedly in the ribs as he lay unconscious: two Irishmen were involved, and it was part of a local feud. The main culprit, John Quinn, shouted to the witness against him, 'I'll mark you missis when I come out!'

The overall conclusion about these acts of street violence suggest a growing problem of social order, common to the West Riding towns as they struggled to cope with waves of new immigrants, massive population growth, and more intensely concentrated groups of people living in poor, often inadequate accommodation.

CHAPTER 18

A London Murder resolved at Triangle
1866

he story of John Jeffrey, the tailor who murdered his own son, is one that is baffling in the bare telling of the truly awful killing of the boy, but which becomes at least partly explicable in the long account of the man's preparation for execution at Newgate. The murderer took place in London, at Seven Dials, but Jeffrey fled to Triangle and altered his appearance to such a degree that he could find work in that tiny, lonely spot and become 'invisible' to the law.

He definitely chose a quiet place in which to go to ground. He shaved off his whiskers as well, and let his beard grow long. It would have seemed that he had disappeared and was making ready to be transmuted into another personality, a man working at his trade in the Pennines, and far from crowded London. He found work with John Helliwell, a tailor.

But this story has to be one of the most informative about the workings of conscience. After all, the murder had been particularly heartless, brutal and even ritualistic. Jeffrey read about the murder in the *Halifax Guardian* . It tells of the boy, aged only six years, being hanged in a cellar at Neal's Passage, St Giles; the hands were tied behind the body, and the paper reports on the fact that Jeffrey was known locally as Mad Dick, that he was having an affair with a woman, and that there was some enmity between himself and the grandmother. The boy's grandmother clearly loved him a great deal.

The heart of the matter appears to be that, because of the oppositions created between the grandmother and aunt on the one hand, and the father and mother on the other, the little boy became a focus of his father's resentment, and then this intensified to destructive hatred. Before the murder, Jeffrey had come to take his son from the care of these other relatives, and had done so with some considerable force and not a little threatening behaviour. A constable had been consulted, but the bottom line was that a father had total power over his family in that time. Jeffrey had forcibly abducted the child, even as he had just been peacefully put to bed.

The murder was almost fastidiously efficient: he had tied the hands, and then done the killing as if he were an official executioner, tugging at the legs . The report states that Jeffrey even took a candle and matches with him when he snatched the child and was overheard saying that: 'He was going on a long journey and would never return.'

Now, in Triangle, the monster was overcome with shame, guilt and remorse. The motive and the manner of killing sit at odds, and the behaviour of the killer in the grip of remorse is also somewhat puzzling. But the fact is that he drank long and deeply at the local tavern, trying to deaden the emotional turmoil he was experiencing. He finally resolved to give himself up to the Halifax constabulary. The extended account of his pangs of guilt in the period up to his execution, as reported in a feature in 1896, are fascinating in terms of psychology, and make the modern reader want to know more about the origin of Jeffrey's nick-name of Mad Dick.

He was seen on 8 September by Sir Henry Edwards, Major Standsfield and Mr Shaw at the West Riding Court and then sent to London for trial. After trying to renounce the first confession, he reverted to the original statement and from then on his story is one of a man wanting to hasten his death. Of course, he was given the death sentence by Mr Justice Wells and sent to Newgate. Jeffrey's pattern of confession, exclamations of being spiritually lost, and begging for some kind of grace, follow the pattern of much criminal popular literature of the time; in the end, after confronting his relatives and intending actions for the expiation of his sins, he was placed in the condemned cell.

Here, the wider social history impinges on this hasty tale: the roughs and blades around the place campaigned to scream and hoot at him, from the cell to the scaffold. He was ready for death but could not cope with the massive crowd's treatment of him. The whole account of his walk to the drop was couched in terms of that whole ceremonial of contrition so prominent at public hangings: 30,000 prayer books were distributed to the crowd of 20,000 people gathered to watch him die.

One sentence in the full report of his death leaves the historian longing for the opposite to be asserted: 'He left no writing of any kind behind him, no.... any special requests of relations.' It was a child-murder clearly of some notoriety in that suburb of the city, but some knowledge of his mind-set, influences and the story behind the given motive would add another dimension to this intriguing story.

The enduring mystery, and one that makes the tale read like a melodramatic Penny Dreadful, is the culprit's desperate attempt to go 'to ground' and then to be unable to tolerate the guilt and remorse eating away at him inside as he tried the buried life of the wrongdoer, being a re-invented identity for such a short time.

CHAPTER 19

Todmorden Tragedy
1868

I n this year, St Mary's vicarage in the town saw a scene of violent slaughter, and injury eventually leading to three deaths, and all done in revenge by a thwarted lover. Reading the account of the young man's assault on the vicarage and the family and servants inside, the events trace a catalogue of brutality, determined physical attack, and outright barbaric killing.

The vicarage at Todmorden, where Weatherill went berserk. The author

The young man who perpetrated the terrible crime was Miles Weatherill, a weaver of the town who lived with his mother and sister in Back Brook Street. When the Rev. Anthony John Plow, the Vicar of Todmorden, employed a young woman from York, Sarah Bell, as a housemaid, Weatherill fell in love with her. They courted openly, and the vicar was obviously fearful and scandalised by this, for he sacked the girl and sent her home to East Yorkshire. That was the kernel of this story of vengeful murder.

Weatherill went all the way home with Sarah and began to express his extreme discontent at the actions of Mr Plow. He was boiling with indignation, and revenge was in his heart. Sarah did find another post, closer to home in York, and Miles wrote to her, talking about the pain he felt at losing her, and blaming it all entirely on the vicar.

One day, Miles went to visit his beloved, and it was on the evening of that day, when he returned, that the outrage occurred. He had left Sarah with a present of a locket, but had insisted on talking in terms of vengeance and called Mr Plow a

Back Brook Street, Todmorden, where the killer lived. The author

'traitor'. His determination to wreak total havoc is evident from his behaviour. He stopped at the Black Swan for a whisky and a little later the servants at the vicarage heard a disturbance in the yard. When Mr Plow himself went out to investigate, the furious attack began and was sustained for some time.

Unbelievably, Miles Weatherill was carrying four pistols and a hatchet. But his weapons were not well primed. When the vicar approached, he fired a shot but it failed, with just the cap exploding: Mr Plow took hold of the young man and a prolonged fight began. In this assault, Miles swung the hatchet at the older man several times, and the vicar called out for help. The attacker had fastened a door, but two men cut this and came on to try to help. Two women, Jane Smith and Elizabeth Spinks were already trying to help their master, and again Weatherill tried to fire a pistol – his last available now as he had dropped two – but again failed, and Mr Plow escaped over a wall.

While Plow had reached safety at the house of his organist, Greenwood, Weatherill now attacked the nurse with the

The Black Swan, *Todmorden, where Weatherill took some Dutch courage before the attack.* The author

hatchet and struck her several times, then he followed her and shot her dead. After this he went upstairs after Mrs Plow, who had recently given birth and was in bed, with her young child. He was now carrying a long and dangerous poker and had been shouting in a rage, 'Where's my Sarah?' before that.

He was begged not to enter the wife's room, but he shouted that he knew exactly what he wanted, and pressed on regardless. Mrs Plow was covered with the bedclothes and he tugged at them. Miles now took up some clothes at the foot of the bed and fired a shot. Again, he was incompetent in this and missed, the bullet ricocheting harmlessly away. In trying to escape into a recess, the vicar's wife was struck hard by the poker and tried to protect her head with her hands. He still belaboured her with the awful weapon and her hands dropped: her feigning death made him at last desist.

It must have been the case that the fury ebbed quickly, and after this last assault, Miles gave himself up to the Parish Clerk, George Stansfield and then was given to a constable. The authorities found lots of ammunition on him, together with a letter from his beloved Sarah. The young man was like a walking ammunition supply, provisioned as if he were to take on a gang of malefactors, rather than a clergyman and his defenceless family. But he coolly tried to light a pipe and then later that night was troubled that he had not fully concluded the slaughter he had intended to do. It is clear that for many days there had been just one murderous thought filling his waking hours. Miles Weatherill was taken to Manchester gaol to be hanged on 4 April that same year.

The two deaths that occurred following that of the poor nurse were Mr Plow himself, and then the young baby. Only after this time had passed did the hard heart yield and the killer wrote to a friend that 'I wish I could undo the shocking crime...'

Of all the homicidal cases recounted here, this has to be the most purely vengeful: a brooding, deeply resentful act that went from defiance to open, planned and bloody murder. His behaviour in custody suggests that for a period he had been like a man possessed, and only came back into conscious awareness of his rage a considerable time after being captured and spoken to by the professionals of the day.

CHAPTER 20

Anonymous Witness to Horrors
1875

In 1953, a mysterious package was discovered by staff at the *Halifax Guardian*. Apparently, it was a large batch of papers, much of the material concerned with ordinary, everyday data about the town. Yet, inside this documentation there was a bundle of fascinating stories on the crime of the nineteenth century. The date of the package was 1875, and it was simply handed in at the counter: the author is still unknown.

The *Courier* reporter in 1953 quoted a famous historian of Halifax, TW Hanson, as saying that there is 'probably no other similar manuscript in existence.' There is a core of material relating to serious crime, notably a crime we might arguably claim was committed by the law: it concerns the maltreatment of a thief who was ordered to submit to a public flogging by the Quarter Sessions. He was supposed to be flogged from the *Waterhouse Arms* to the *Upper George Inn*, but it went wrong, and the wretch was dragged. Men whipped the horse so hard that it broke into a gallop and the thief was dragged around Bull Green and George Street, men unable to get near him with a whip.

But the writer also tells of the hanging of a coiner. A woolcomber called Iredale was hanged at York for the offence of clipping the coin of the realm, and the anonymous author reports that Iredale, who lived at Bank Bottom, Southowram, was brought home with the noose still around his neck, and his wife displayed the corpse at the charge of a penny to each person who came to look.

The manuscript clearly gives a series of images of criminal life in the early to mid nineteenth century, and the data illustrate the hard, unfeeling nature of many people at the time. Most notable here is the story of Jonathan Walsh of

Bull Green today. Once, thieves were whipped and flogged as they passed through here. The author

Blackledge. He was a miser living at Cold Well Hill at Southowram. His crime was to bury his wife outside of consecrated ground, simply burying her in his own fields. But retribution came when he himself died. He had said that he wanted to be buried at the highest point on his own land with his head above ground. In actual fact, the coffin slipped out of place when they were trying to carry out his wishes, so his legs were highest.

The men involved left the coffin that way, and so the miser was eventually paid back for his lack of respect given to his wife. It seems that Blackledge was a man with a nature to match his name.

The pack of papers became an unusual source for the social history of crime in this era, and the depiction of the hard execution of the law given here confirms the Dickensian view

The Upper George *where various hearings took place, and whose yard involved the punishment of felons.* The author

of the desperate plight of the criminal underclass, spanning images not unlike Hogarth's 'Gin Lane' and Dickens' own paupers grubbing in the Thames silt for rubbish worth a few farthings. Halifax in that Regency to early Victorian period was a tough place to live and no mistake – especially if you wandered onto the wrong side of the law.

When discovered, the only nagging doubt in the journalists' minds must have been that it was on the day of 1 April. But there was nothing foolish about this record of astonishing brutality and toughness in a period of relentless social change, when the weak went under, into anonymity.

CHAPTER 21

Mysterious Death of a Woman
1876

Ambler Jagger kept a boarding house in Halifax, at Barrack tavern. Luckily, he recognised the body of a young woman found dead near Brighouse in a quarry. Otherwise, she was unknown in the area, and her death was a mystery.

What was known is that, while walking in the open country, and been seen in the main street of Greetland and on the road to Brighouse later, she met three factory hands, young men who, it transpired, took her to a cabin 'for an immoral purpose'. She was Sarah Ann Wood, thirty one, and had been living as a prostitute. She had asked them the way to Halifax, and after walking with her for some way, they ended up in the cabin nor far from Robinson's quarry, and left her there.

Poor Sarah only had one eye and sight with the other was impaired. She had lived a hard life, and had served a term in

The centre of Greetland now, where Sarah Wood was seen before her fateful meeting near Brighouse. The author

prison, and had been living in Halifax for the previous year. Why she was so far away remains unknown. But it was a fateful meeting, and the coroner at the time was troubled by the actions of the young men. Had it been a 'business' meeting for Sarah and the men, or had there been foul play?

Much depended on the accounts given of the body, and there was plenty of such information. She had been found by William Duckworth, a steam-crane tenter, at the bottom of a fairly deep shaft. As it was unfenced, it was first assumed that she had lost her way, and with her poor eyesight, had fallen victim to the fall in the dark. Ben Allen and Bottomley Kershaw brought the corpse out, and had much to say about its condition at the time. Her face was on her arm, resting downwards, and no-one was sure what blood was evident.

The surgeon, Henry Pritchett, added a lot more. Here, things become cloudy regarding any previous assault. There were several bruises on one hand, another below the elbow and a large bruise on her face. As these were all on her right side, it was thought that they were caused by a fall on stones. It seemed that there was no detail suggesting that she had been murdered, even though it was said that she was a strong, muscular woman, and no bones were broken.

A constable Bell had arrested two of the young men, Wilson and Allan, but that later testimony exonerated them. It took a long time to gather witnesses and for enough factual statement to be taken as to their innocence; but ultimately, despite a verdict of accidental death, there are unanswered questions about Sarah's wanderings, and what exactly happened that day. She was certainly given money, but what else happened, and whether assaults took place, forensic science was not equal to the task in 1876.

It was a sad, unresolved story, complicated by the fact that it involved a 'fallen woman' and several young men who were well 'in their drink' that day. Although several people saw her, and knew things about her, the fact remains that this was a young woman whose life had fallen apart – not only had her health suffered, but most of her family were dead also. Clearly, she drifted around, maybe earning money in the only way she knew, and risking her life in that lifestyle.

CHAPTER 22

Manslaughter at Dean Clough
1876

his story places the famous sufferings of Smike, in Charles Dickens's *Nicholas Nickleby*, in realistic historical perspective, because these actual acts of cruelty on a boy drove him to his death, totally in the power of a superior at his place of work. The story reminds us that, in Victorian times, children were chattels in the engines of industry, sacrificed to economic forces.

Of all the stories of cruelty and man's inhumanity to man encountered in reviewing the social history of crime in Halifax, none displays such a harrowing account of callous maltreatment than that inflicted on the miserable nine year old doffer at Crossley's, Dean Clough, Peter Keegan.

Keegan was repeatedly abused and physically assaulted by Harry Crowther, an overlooker, and even the threat of legal action by the father of the young boy, Patrick Keegan, could do nothing to stop the relentless violence done to the victim. The attacks culminated in a severe blow inflicted on the young man's head as he was thrown against the end of the rollers in the mill. Later medical reports said that there were 'copious discharges from the boy's nostrils' after that, and that he suffered agonising headaches for several days before he received any medical attention.

The Keegans, of Sunnyside Street, Range Lane, seem very patient and forebearing by modern standards, only giving a rather too co-operative statement after the first crisis, when the violence was becoming only too apparent: 'Don't beat him any more. If he does anything wrong, send him home and I will try to do something with him' said the father. Of course, the context is a time when the boy's wage would have been essential to maintain the family solvency. The tragic heart of this story is that, from his first complaint that Harry Crowther

Dean Clough. Inside here, ruthless men like Crowther could beat children to death as part of their work. The author

had hit him with a lifter's strap to the death at home several days later, young Peter Keegan had kept going to work, doing long and exhausting hours with a severe headache.

The *Guardian* report gives a dramatic and heart-rending image of the victim at the worst point: 'Deceased had been complaining of his head all day, and between ten and eleven he got on his knee in bed and said, 'It's not me... oh dear, oh

Harry, it's not me...' At the inquest, after such testimony, it was time to arraign Crowther, and he appeared at the inquest on the Monday after a weekend break.

Crowther was brought before J D Hutchinson on a charge of manslaughter and remanded in custody, with a huge bail at that time of £100. Dr Dolan's post mortem examination revealed, in minute detail, an account of severe brain damage, with an excess of a watery fluid and a serum discharge. Otherwise, other organs were healthy. But 'there was no external mark of injury on the head or other parts of the body', and with that crucially important detail, Harry Crowther was released to do further mindless violence on young doffers at the mill. A brutal sadist was still working in a position of power which allowed him to maltreat children at his own whims and moods.

The first sign of real trouble had been Peter's sister, running home very upset, and reporting the violence on her brother. But nothing was done, and the law allowed this cruelty to go unpunished, after a young boy had endured a slow and very painful death. The inquest at the *Coach and Horses*, Haley Hill, must have been a solemn affair.

CHAPTER 23

Puzzling Death at the Infirmary
1878

Now we would be crying 'police brutality' but the case of William Redman of Back Chapeltown, shows that the problems of coping with the 'drunk and disorderly' have always been complicated for the police. In fact, all the evidence points to a sad story of a man with internal injuries being assumed to be intoxicated, and bundled into a police cell. The night there appears to have been the decisive factor in his death in the Halifax Infirmary the day after.

Redman was a labourer working for the Corporation. He had always been a healthy man, but on the Sunday of this fateful week he started complaining of having dizzy spells to his wife. William Robinson had been working with Redman on

The Royal Halifax Infirmary, where Redman died after being ignored in the cells.
The author

the Monday, and had even had breakfast with his workmate. He said that Redman had only drunk coffee, and had been unable to eat anything. Then, later that morning, he saw Redman keel over and his pick fell to the ground.

He managed to eat some food at the *Mason's Arms*, and then, while feeling very unwell, insisted on walking home alone. This is where the problems really started. Another friend, one George Salmon, a dyer, saw Redman at North Bridge by the Pineapple corner, and tried to force him to be taken home. Redman had fallen to the ground, a crowd gathered, and two constables, Abbot and Rew, carried him to a cell.

In contemporary terms, what happened next has to put the blame on the police, but they were hard pressed, as thirteen drunken people had spent time in that cell throughout the day. Four visits were made to Redman. Sometimes he slept and other times he was awake and vomited. In terms of the year 1878, it would be unreasonable to argue that the delay by the law officers in finding medical attention for Redman caused his death. But the fact is that he was taken hurriedly to the infirmary, and later died there.

The Princess Mary ward, where Redman went, taken on the day of its demolition in June 2003. The author

The only complication is that he was badly bruised. So did he fall or was he pushed? He had been perceived as being drunk and disorderly, and as a matter of routine, some force would have been used by the two arresting officers. When Redman's daughter came to see him in the cell, she was turned away as he was said to be asleep. In fact, it appears that he was in a coma.

The coroner, William Barstow, had a very busy time in this year, but he had the common sense to say, in delivering his verdict that 'the police should be strongly advised to use every possible means to ascertain whether persons locked up are only drunk, or otherwise seriously ill.' It does seem alarming that, in the course of writing the report, the journalist concerned had referred to no less than six police officers, and yet William Redman was assumed drunk throughout the day. The verdict was that he had died of 'apoplexy' – a term used throughout the nineteenth century to cover hundreds of different cerebral illnesses.

CHAPTER 24

Suicide at North Bridge
1878

Benjamin Dowse, a worker at Crossley's, Dean Clough, when asked by his wife why he had hurled himself from North bridge into the river, said , 'I couldn't help it... I couldn't help it... it's all because of the studying.' But there was much more wrong with the unfortunate young man, and he died later that day in the infirmary.

Dowse, who had been living in Victoria Street, Haley Hill, was thirty years old, and a roller coverer by trade. He was both physically and mentally ill, having been sick and away from work for several months, and a Mr Kirby's assistant, a pharmacist, said he was suffering from congestion of the lungs.

The poor man had been having hallucinations, complaining of a numbness at the top of his skull, and amazingly for a case such as this, he was a teetotaller who had in fact taken a dislike to beer and told his wife that 'taking bitter beer' was for him a

Haley Hill, near to Benjamin Dowse's home. The author

'punishment.' There is clearly a deep malaise here in the case of a suicide who took such desperate measures, as North Bridge, now seen below the flyover across the valley from the Bradford direction, was then twenty five yards above the water, and the water was shallow, as a man who helped bring Dowse out, clinging on to life, reported some important details.

This was Mr Absalom Walshaw, who was given the alarm by a carpet weaver from Ovenden, David Smith, who actually saw Dowse come down on the west side, near Bowling Dyke. The men on the scene gave Dowse brandy and used a ladder as a stretcher, taking care to keep his head above the water.

Elizabeth Wood, daughter of George Wood, the landlord of *The Flying Dutchman*, also saw Dowse on the bridge, and from her testimony it seems as though he deliberated, lifting one leg over and then pausing, but she said that finally 'he seemed determined to throw himself and was not looking over, and so overbalanced himself.'

One of the most interesting features of the story is just how much help was there, and how many citizens strenuously tried to help the poor man. After all, it was a long drop to shallow water, and anyone in command of their faculties would have known that such a desperate attempt would most likely not end in a quick and painless death. Several townsfolk were speedily on the scene and Dowse was cared for in his miserable plight.

Calderdale, of course, has a plentiful supply of streams, becks and canals, and the Victorian newspapers and journals often carry stories of

A view from above the North Bridge, showing the drop Dowse suffered. The author

people under stress attempting suicide by drowning. Most were remarkably successful, and many had more clear-cut reasons that Dowse. But his remark about 'studying' stands out as a rare and very individual detail in the death of this young family man.

His dying was considerably painful, as the surgeon reported that Dowse had a compound fracture of the right thigh and also of the right leg, with severe injuries to his face as well. Dowse was a family man, obviously under great mental and emotional strain and most likely so because he had been unable to work due to his lung disease. All he had on his person when searched by the police officer was a small sum of money and a child's birth certificate.

The verdict returned was 'suicide while in a state of temporary insanity.' There was also a long discussion on the possible construction of a parapet on the bridge. This was not done. Still there today, in blue and gold, North Bridge looks attractive beneath the massive and functional concrete of modern road-structures. But it has its ghosts and its boards have been trodden by some sad, distracted souls from the satanic mills of that time.

North Bridge today, topped by the fly-over spanning Dean Clough. Dowse's fall would have been onto stone, with very shallow water. The author

CHAPTER 25

Murderer Trapped
1888

Some men on the run take every risk possible, and seem to relish displaying that bravado associated with a kind of desperation which is close to flouting the law, trying to dupe and cajole anyone trying to see them for what they are.

Such extraordinary bravado was shown by Will Jackson, a dangerous runaway killer from Strangeways in 1888 who was eventually caught on the Halifax road out of Brighouse after weeks on the run across Lancashire and Yorkshire. He had been brazen and bold in the extreme, even robbing people he had known in the past en route for what he thought was safety.

The story begins when Jackson was taken by a warder called Webb to an upper room in the matron's building in

The road by the bridge and the Black Bull, *Brighouse, where Jackson was apprehended.* The author

Strangeways. He was supposed to be doing some plumbing work, but exploited the situation in which he was given a hammer, to kill his guard and make a daring escape through the roof to freedom.

Jackson took socks and boots from the dead warder, and then committed two burglaries in Lancashire: in Oldham he first took some clothes from one house, and then broke into the home of a Captain Wood of the Salvation Army. What he did there illustrates the foolhardy and somewhat twisted nature of the man, as he left a note:

Goodbye Captain. Though lost to sight, to memory dear.
Shakespeare.

He took money, and unbelievably left the warder's socks at Wood's home. The chase was on, and the killer with a sense of humour was to become also a bizarre public performer while on the run.

He turned up at an inn and sang several popular songs, and also advertised the fact that he was supposed to be going to Wakefield to do some masonry work. With characteristic sick bravado, he met with a man called Whitehead, and on being asked about the building work, produced the trowel and said, after playing with the instrument for a while, 'How would you like it in you?' His humour was on the borderline between sick and anarchic.

Seldom has an escaped killer travelled so far and been sighted so many times. Calling at several public houses, he eventually arrived at Leeds, then the police let the Marsden law enforcement know that Jackson was on the move towards Calderdale or Kirklees. He was seen asleep at one point, outside the Springhead Parsonage. At a hotel called *The Lighthouse* he did his singing performance and was apparently well dressed, having had his shoes recently cleaned and he was wearing dark clothes and a white shirt. It seems that he had been earning or stealing money while on the move.

If it wasn't for the fact that Jackson was a cold-blooded killer, one could comment that he becomes almost likeable as his saga unfolds. He appears to have ate and drank his way across the Pennines, at one point being sick over his shoes (hence the note about them being clean later on) and openly bragged about his drinking prowess as he arrived at each new place.

His first robbery on the run led him to take half a gallon of porter and a box of cigars: that would slow down most men, but he kept on, evading his pursuers and shifting quickly and unpredictably from place to place. One might conclude that he purposely left clues and hints as he travelled on, almost teasing the officers on the watch for him. He was reputedly a striking figure, though short (about five feet six) and had a buoyant personality. He was the life and soul of the party, but with the small footnote that he was likely to kill someone if the drink took hold.

His luck finally ran out one night as he walked into Halifax from Brighouse, where he had been seen not far from the bridge. But even to the very last detail of this remarkable chase, it is recorded that he had been supposedly sighted in Sunderland and in Barnsley not long before he surfaced on that road and was taken to Dewsbury to be charged. *The Strangeways Pimpernel* would seem to be a suitable sub-title for this escapade's hero. The name Will Jackson doesn't have that dashing romantic ring to it, but he taunted his pursuers and flaunted his rash defiance with humour and contempt as he continued the journey towards inevitable recapture.

Given the chance, Jackson, one feels, could have written a lively autobiography.

CHAPTER 26

Death of Two Lovers
1888

The sad story of Harry Evans and Ann Pickles is one of those cases which is open to several interpretations. Evans lived with his parents at Springfield Street and Ann was a farmer's daughter from Jug Head. They were both eighteen years old, had been in love, and both were found drowned, but in different places. His body was found in a reservoir near Black Dike Mills, and she in a water-trough with an apparent suicide note. The note is what the extreme doubt of the case rests on, making it uncertain whether she drowned herself or whether Harry killed her. This is the note:

> *When you find me, read this to my mother. I told harry what you said and you heard about him but you did not like it and said it wasn't right. It caused him to say he would not go with me and this drove me mad But tell him to forgive me for what I have done for I couldn't help it. Harry You're the first that's ever gone with me and you shall be the last.*

Now, according to the girl's father, she had never been to school and was illiterate. The errors in spelling and punctuation here indicate someone either with a basic literacy and able to use sentences, or a complete forgery. In other words, it was most likely written by Harry. It was found on top of a wall, under a stone, near where Ann's body lay on its back in the trough.

The trigger for some kind of passionate argument was almost certainly the fact that Harry was about to become a father – but the mother was a young woman from Thornton who had been causing problems. Harry had refused to see this girl again, and wanted only Ann. He had been seen in the streets with other young men as normal; he was upset on the night that the Thornton girl had visited and caused a row, and he had left the house, not returning, saying that he would 'take action in the matter.' His body was dragged from the reservoir in the early hours of the next day.

The woman who laid out Ann's corpse only reported purple marks across the waist. No mention of any marks incriminating Harry was made at the inquest at the *King's Arms Inn*, Queensbury in front of Mr Barstow J P. But no decision could be made about the cause of her death. The open verdict leaves no end of questions, and the suicide note was perhaps most logically the product of Harry. However, one has to note that drowning in a horse-trough could easily be done to someone with very little pressure and no marks would necessarily be evident in those times of no real forensic testing. This all seems most likely if the woman's illiteracy were true. Her sister said that there was never a pencil in the house, and that Ann used to spell out the letters of words in the newspaper and her brother would tell her the meanings.

The suicide note was written at a table, by someone who knew their sentences and at least enough English to write something unambiguous. No doubt Sherlock Holmes would call this murder, followed by the suicide of the young and tragic killer, Harry Evans. But the truth will never be known, and the phrase of 'They died for love' will stick to the sad story.

The only sure knowledge here is that, whatever really happened late that night in the fields, the emotions raging at the heart of the relationship led to two wasteful deaths, and a tangled web had clearly been made by the doomed young woman from Jug Head, suffering a horrible death. Several relationships were cut short that fateful night.

CHAPTER 27

Playing at Jack the Ripper
1889

Jack the Ripper committed five murders in the East End of London between 31 August 1888 and 9 November 1888. It is well documented that, as with all major high-profile media-centred murders, not only the 'copycat' crimes tend to come along, but also the other secondary incidents and events, such as the numerous letters and confessions the police received. But in Halifax, very shortly after Jack's last killing, one Frederick Brett (clearly a deranged individual) was one of those influenced by the notorious killer.

Having said that, to call the murder he did something with an 'influence' is to give some kind of perverted credit where it

The Halifax railway station, where Brett was a labourer. The author

is not due. For the fact is that Brett was an unbalanced, dangerous man with a slender grasp of reality. His crime was something apparently integral to his brutal personality, and murdering his wife was no surprise when the story of his temperament and habits is told.

Brett was a railway labourer in Halifax, and he had a drink problem. The station and line at Halifax was until recent times a grim place, always a dour environment, and with the Victorian management of the railways came much casual labour (down the road at Luddenden Foot, Branwell Bronte had had problems keeping to the rules and also had difficulties keeping his job). The responsibilities bring along with them a range of regulations and all the ancillary work involved in keeping the trains running involves responsibility and maturity. These qualities Brett clearly lacked.

He tended to indulge his fondness for ale too easily and then become possessed by rages; often these would be a show of temper with his workmates; at times he would be moody. One colleague notes that he saw Brett playing with a knife,

A view of the old platform beneath the new buildings at the station, where Brett would have worked, usually drunk. The author

throwing it to the ground near his own feet. There were deep and complex struggles about his sense of self down beneath the moods and the boozing. The turning-point, switching him from a temperamental man to a husband possessed by jealousy came when his wife was too friendly and forthcoming to some workmates in the local: he simmered his hatred and rage, now with a focus for the pent-up violence. There was devilry in his heart, and he was focused on one final act of murder. The coldness is in the mundane build-up to the actual knifing.

Arriving home one night, his intention clear in his mind, he ate his tea and apparently allowed some small-talk before he unleashed his temper on her, slitting her throat with a small clasp-knife. There was none of the high dignity of Othello: merely an insane homicidal urge while 'in his cups'.

Frederick Brett was just thirty nine when he did this terrible thing. He was hanged at Leeds gaol by the famous executioner, James Billington, noted for his taciturnity and deep-set eyes, unmoved and professional as he sent men to their doom. Brett was executed along with another wife-killer, one Robert West, who had done exactly the same thing to his wife, and for the very same reasons.

Brett's statement to the police seems totally deranged, if not manically sick, as it was simply, 'Yes, I have done it and it can't be undone. I was only playing at Jack the Ripper.' There was surely never such a sickly irony than this 'copy-cat' homicide.

CHAPTER 28

Shot for a Shilling
1890

Patrick Morley had a serious character-flaw. He had no control over his fists. Time and time again he struck his wife, and finally she left him. Morley was Irish, an immigrant who had left everything and everyone behind at home and tried to make a new life in Yorkshire. But the story of his decline is depressingly familiar: from drink to violence, to more drink, and then the final tragedy. He had settled for the usual fate of such immigrants – to be 'general labourer', working hard at tough physical graft, and drinking heavily when he wasn't working.

He was a moody man, unable to keep a job for long, and having trouble with every relationship he was involved in. His wife, Elizabeth, tended to be the closest to him in his

Once a favourite haunt of killer Patrick Morley, a yard off George Square. The author

The desperate Morley used to be seen here, across George Square, often 'in his cups' and violent. In 1890, he had his murderous thoughts here. The author

tempers, and closest to his fists. She stood this for some considerable time, but enough was enough and she left him. She just walked out and let him simmer and boil and hopefully to take the frustration out on himself, not on her.

Morley begged her to return. He tried this on several occasions and even sent some associates to put his case. But this was to no purpose. He had to accept that he had driven her away. What would he do then, but drink? He drank more than ever, and the dark thoughts led to the notion that she had deeply wronged him and that she should suffer.

In court, his defence's argument that everything had been an accident didn't wash: he had a gun when he called on Elizabeth on 21 September and everything pointed to the fact that the bullet was meant for her. The amazing detail in the story is that Morley called on her to do no more than to try to prise a shilling out of the poor woman. She unwisely refused, and he pulled the gun on her and shot her dead. He was very drunk on this visit, and aggressive, his moods changing manically from threats to pleading. But inevitably, everything led to the gun being produced.

He appeared before Mr Justice Grantham and the plea was insanity, and then as a second, supporting line of thought, that the gun had gone off accidentally. The whole trial defence strategy smacks of sheer desperation. But there was too much corroborating evidence and testimony that Patrick Morley was a violent man with a deep, rankling grudge. The summing –up of the judge was notably in support of the prosecution, with these facts in mind.

Patrick Morley was hanged at Leeds, by James Billington. It had been a familiar story of decline and desperation, leading relentlessly to the scaffold, and all over the loan of a shilling. Never was a refused loan surely so dire in the consequences. But whether Elizabeth could have saved her life by giving him the money is an open question. Somehow, imagining that gun in his pocket, one has to think that he was intent on ending her life, whatever happened. If ever a man made an excuse for himself, in order to kill, it was this case.

CHAPTER 29

The Ackrigg Case
1894

High up on the moors of Blackstone Edge in December, 1894, there would be very few travellers on the road, and no-one taking a long walk just for the exercise. It makes sense, therefore, that Peter McIntyre, the landlord of *The Wagon and Horses* inn in that lonely spot, expected a quiet night as he sat in his tavern, the place shrouded in fog. No-one coming from the Lancashire direction had called in that day, and he didn't even expect local company, as there is no other settlement within a mile of the inn.

But around seven o'clock a stranger came through the cold, foggy night. It was a man, and he was quiet, moody. He ordered three pennorth of whisky and sat in the tap-room. He was served by the servant, Eliza, who gave him his drink and then left him alone by the fire. But the man was clearly restless and disturbed about something. More than once he stood up, as if intending to do something, and then returned to his seat. His glance kept going to the door, as if he was expecting someone coming after him.

The first sign of a problem came when he finally got to his feet and approached the landlady, asking her if she had a stray dog tethered there. Mrs McIntyre was obviously troubled by this, and was beginning to worry about this nervous stranger, but she said that there was no such animal there. Then the man gave a sharp and threatening reply:

Yes you have... you have a stray dog fastened up here belonging to me. Shack, of Walsden, told me so.

By now things were looking dark and unsettled as the weather outside, and the seemingly peaceful evening beginning to judder with apprehension. Mr McIntyre was called to assist, and he came to talk to the man, repeating that he had no dog of his at the inn. McIntyre walked away from the stranger, thus turning his back to him as he walked towards the kitchen. At that point, the man pulled a gun from his pocket and said , 'This is the dog!' He brandished a so-called 'bull-dog' revolver, and shot Mr McIntyre in the shoulder.

Mrs McIntyre had tried to rush and knock the man over before he could fire, but failed, and amazingly, although he now pointed his weapon at her and shot, she was saved by her corsetry. One of the busks in her corset, being made of steel, stopped the ball, and although with the first impact she cried that she was 'done', very soon she saw that she was unhurt. Now the couple ran for the kitchen and bolted themselves in. Although there was a gun in the house there was no ammunition, and of course there was no-one living near who might be summoned.

The man was seemingly completely insane, and as they shivered in fear in the kitchen, he slammed his fists hard on the door, threatening to blow out their brains. The only option was to run for it, out on the moor. They opened the kitchen window, despite McIntyre now being very seriously wounded, and they ran for somewhere to hide out in the cold night, followed by poor Eliza. But Eliza, instead of lying down flat and praying that the madman would not arrive, took off her clogs and ran towards Littleborough. The man saw her and ran after her, finally grabbing hold of her and demanded to know where the others were. In abject fear, she told him.

He held his gun to her head and said, 'Now for your life … where is the money?'

Eliza told him that it was upstairs, so he let her go and repeated his vow that he would kill her if he saw her again. She moved as fast as she could towards Castle Farm and when she reached there, totally collapsed.

The terrified McIntyres were all this time lying flat on the icy ground, wondering if he would appear at any second behind them and finish them off. From where they were, they saw him return to the inn, look through the kitchen window and then climb in. This was the point at which their luck turned, as by sheer chance, a sound of a trap could be heard. It was two men coming home from a day's shooting – a Mr Ormorod of Walsden and Mr Heap of Littleborough. They heard the cries of Mrs McIntyre and ran to her. She was soon safely in their cart, and they drove to bring the law officers from Littleborough.

The police and doctor came, but found that the man had gone, leaving the house ransacked. He had seemingly found nothing worth his while, as there was £50 still there, together with articles of jewellery. Everything pointed to the fact that the madman had been disturbed and scampered off into the night.

Some information about the man then emerged. He had set off to Halifax but had been lost and was tracked down the next day at Derby Bar. He was one Robert Ackrigg, who had been living in Todmorden for some time, but was originally from the Lake District. He was a hardened criminal with a long record, being discharged from Walton Gaol only two days before he arrived at the *Wagon and Horses*. His previous crimes had included horse stealing and burglary. At the Manchester Assizes on 2 February, he was tried for the attempted murder of the publicans, and was sentenced to twelve years penal servitude.

At the trial, the man they had thought completely crazed and manic on that awful night put on a performance of madness for the benefit of the court, trying to chew at his own clothing. This had started even before the trial, as he was detained in Littleborough. But it was all to no avail. The remarkable thing about this is that his 'playing Hamlet' in the gaol and then in court is in keeping with his performance in the inn. For it reads that way – with him sitting and watching the door in fear, while he could be seen by the landlady. Everything points to his being a consummate actor, calculating on his actions being interpreted as those of a madman from his first appearance on that dark night on the moors. It is as if he was creating a signpost saying, 'Look, this man is insane and not responsible for his actions.'

The brave Mr McIntyre was very badly injured and died a few years after, never having fully recovered from being shot on that cold December night when the madman arrived, asking after his dog.

CHAPTER 30

How 'Fiery' Leah Ackroyd Died
1898

rancis Wood Ackroyd of Wainhouse Terrace, King Cross, was a dyer. He was a 'steady' man who liked a drink but not excessively so. On the face of it, that is not a recipe for a person to be destructive or cruel. But when his wife, Leah and their young son of fourteen months old were found drowned, floating in the canal at Sowerby Bridge, a story emerged of two people dominated by anger, intolerance and threats. It can't have been a happy marriage.

Francis had come home and spoken sharply to his wife when he learned that she had not mended some of his clothes. Her reaction was to run out into the night, taking young Nathaniel with her. At the inquest, held at the *Wharf House Hotel*, it emerged that Leah was a fiery woman and had threatened on more than one occasion to take her own life. She and her husband, who had been married ten years, had always had a tempestuous relationship. But the issue is complicated when further details are added: four years before this awful final act she had quarrelled

The Ackroyds street today, Wainhouse Road, King Cross. The author

passionately with her sister (who lived in Barnsley) and the sister had struck Leah on the head with a coffee canister. The court considered the fact that her temper was notably shorter after this, and that she became increasingly irascible. It was noted that her relationship with her other child, eight years old at the time of her death, had also been strained.

Francis said that she had several times dashed off into the night in a mood, and sometimes threatened to kill herself, but that she had always come back. On this fatal evening, though, he had threatened to hit her –something he swore he had only ever done once before, and that was eight years before this event, after she had thrown a cup at him. A neighbour saw her standing on her house steps, holding the child. She offered Leah a shawl, which she took before going towards Sowerby.

The neighbour, a Mrs Emily Graves, had often heard the pair quarrel, but disagreed that Francis was 'a drunkard'; he seemed to be a reliable worker. In the past the couple had suffered hard times, and Leah, thirty seven at the time of her death, had done extra work such as washing and cleaning when she and Francis were going through this tough period in their marriage. There had been stresses and strains, and the general view of her was that she was irritable, contrary and temperamental.

But on that June night, it was the last straw. Maybe she had suffered brain damage that four years earlier; it could be that she feared that Francis would strike her again; but her life appears to have been, as they say in Yorkshire, 'ruled wi't'moon' – somehow destined to some kind of personal tragedy. In court, when it was said that she had left home in a temper on earlier occasions that she had once stayed with her neighbour, there was even time for a joke, as the lawyer asked if Francis was a good husband and added, 'Not as good as yours I dare say.' Even with a subject as distressing as this, a court has time for jocularity.

But the end of her life was indeed dismal and heart-rendingly sad: she was seen about fifty yards down from the canal bridge, floating in the muddy water, with her little son tied to her and the line fastened with two safety-pins. She was seen and retrieved by David Thomas, a labourer living in

Emily Graves had seen Leah weeping here, close to what is now the busy junction at King Cross, with Wainhouse Tower behind. The author

Sowerby Bridge. When asked what the deceased was wearing when found, Thomas simply said that he would say she was a 'respectable woman'. It looks like a case of two people unable to live together without harmony, and that divisions in the family inevitably came through. It was all too much for poor Leah.

CHAPTER 31

Riot in Brighouse
1900

There were many in 1900, at the height of the Boer War, who were seriously and noisily opposed to the ideology of Imperialism then so prominent in the media propaganda. The Golden Jubilee was still recent in their minds, wars had been fought in South Africa against various tribes, and in India there was constant confrontation. On 29 May that year Brighouse was one of the centres of disturbance, and it proved to be nasty, violent and brutal.

The cue for such feelings was ostensibly the death of the first Brighouse soldier killed in the Boer War – Private Sam Wilkinson who died at Ladysmith in January, 1900. After the relief of Ladysmith in February, there was a large-scale celebration in Brighouse, with a half-day holiday for the schoolchildren and early closing in the mills.

The market square, Brighouse, where trouble began in 1900. The author

But on 29 May the Brighouse Independent Labour Party held a rally against this long-standing British imperialistic doctrine and the Pro-Boers were present. The war had brought about a division across the land, the individual opinion resting on whether or not the knowledge of the Boers being original settlers carried any weight in the argument. The general feeling in the streets was that the Brighouse meeting was for anti-war rhetoric.

It must have been easy to forecast trouble: there were around 300 youths present with the Labour Councillor, Denis Hardaker as John Lister of Shibden Hall began to speak in the market place. He took a hard line on conscription and addressed the question of having a huge army to maintain the Empire. The abuse and the missiles began to be hurled at him. This was only the beginning of a rough and rowdy day.

A succession of speakers then felt the venom of the mob: the Reverend Roberts of Bradford, Ben Riley of Huddersfield and Sam Hemsley, who was Secretary of the Bradford Labour Party. All kinds of objects were thrown, including dead birds and sods of earth. The speakers, walking into Commercial

The tow-path near the market place, perhaps showing what a dangerous place this was for a riot. The author

Street, were followed by the mob, and now things were well out of hand. A substantial body of police arrived on the scene and actually formed a barrier. But Lister, Hemsley and Hardaker were pursued, kicked and abused on Halifax Road. The climax came at Lane Head, when Lister tried to fight back, and was severely beaten; he was trailed by the mob across a considerable area of streets and lanes, finally being almost knocked unconscious.

Hardaker was also physically assaulted, and Lister had to spend some time in a London hospital, such was his condition. No-one was charged with the violent attack on Lister, but a stone mason from Hove Edge, one James Binns, was charged with the assault on Hardaker, escaping with a large fine.

The riot plainly reflected the larger national dissension at a time when the new challenges to the notion of the 'red map of the world' with Britain at the centre were having to contend with deep local feeling, often based on a sense of noble sacrifice or worthless waste. Both views were boiling deep down in the resentment and frustration of the populace, and Brighouse saw the worst side of this on that day in early spring, 1900, when it must have seemed to the local people that the *Riot Act* should have been read.

The bridge by the market: again, part of the route taken by those involved.
The author

CHAPTER 32

The Story of a Christmas Stabbing 1901

There was a great deal of patience required of the three men who heard the convoluted story of the stabbing of Henry Walker by Thomas Mansfield on Christmas Day, 1901. It happened at a time when tempers are out of hand, and celebration soon turns to violence, but there was nothing simple about this, and Walker was slashed across the face in an alley by the *Pineapple* public house.

The three men trying to take it all in – Waterhouse, Pollard and Ralph – must have known that this was a difficult matter when Walker began by saying, 'I was quarrelling with another man when Mansfield came in and threw himself upon me...' The brawl went quiet for a short while, as Walker was shoved through a back door by two protective friends, but then he found the crazed Mansfield coming at him with the knife.

He was seriously cut, and taken to the nearest druggist's shop. It was asserted that Walker was not drunk on this occasion, but his statements were dubious as he was arguing already, before the furore burst upon the scene of goodwill and celebration. Walker, it seems likely, was on a binge in fact: he had been at a cottage cellar party in Park Street for hours before coming to the *Pineapple*, where he met Mansfield and they were friendly at first.

Walker comes across as a sociable man with a lively sense of humour, a raconteur and a wag: he was the sort of man who makes extreme friends, but who also makes both friends and enemies quickly if the mood is on him at the wrong time. This Christmas, as the barrage of questions fired at him in the cross-examination testify, he had perhaps been wandering around from tavern to hotel, apparently arguing with a soldier, and notes that he was surprised that one particular landlord had not called a constable to take him away. Reading between the

Now the Inn-Cognito, *this is close to where the* Pineapple *stood – a public house with dozens of violent stories attached to it.* The author

lines in the text of his statements, it seems that he had very little idea of what he was doing or where he was on this day. Two friends, Goodall and Knowles, had not only moved him from any further confrontations or provocations, but were trying in vain to protect him from his own worst enemy – himself.

Goodall said that he was aware that Walker was fighting with someone in the back kitchen of the hotel, when Mansfield burst through, grabbed Walker, and 'threw him down at the room door.' The tale has the hallmark of a fight with the short allegiances and tempers of men possessed by drink.

This testimony also contradicts Walker's memory, as Goodall said that he took Mansfield and disarmed him after the first attempt to stab Walker. Now, at this point, the magistrates must have been utterly confused as to cause, responsibility, or indeed what the actual course of events in this prolonged ruck must have been.

Finally, one Thomas Lister introduces the possibility of food being the cause, noting that he saw Mansfield slash Walker with the knife, and that blood spilled onto his own clothes, but that there was no food in Mansfield's hands at that time. Mansfield had asked, roughly, if his victim was eating anything, before he attacked.

The solicitor attempting vainly to defend Mansfield eventually tired of the sheer muddle before him and must have accepted, along with everyone else in the room, that a group of drunks had fallen out over something trivial, taken sides like a playground scrap, and then the affair had been intensified into a mob hue and cry, because Lister refers to seeing a crowd in pursuit of Mansfield, and that a whole gang of men had been in the yard at the time when the hapless Walker had been supposedly taken out through a back entrance to steal quietly away from the fracas.

Such brawls go along with Christmas parties, one could argue: but this one got completely out of hand, and spilled out into the street, all because one particular trouble-maker lost control, and another one was probably so out of any kind of self-awareness that he provoked anyone in sight. The magistrates must have longed for the floor-show to end and for normality to return as their New Year of 1902 beckoned. The only mystery is whether or not there was actually a first offence or insult given to someone by someone else; but this, if it existed, is lost in a drunken haze.

Even Thomas Mansfield himself was as confused about this as anyone else.

CHAPTER 33

Sweethearts Shot
1909

Priscilla Milnes, of Hope Street, Halifax, was courting a young man from Siddal, one Arnold Vowles, and they had been 'walking out' for some time as they ambled towards open fields beyond what was the Halifax Zoo and gardens in September, 1909. Poor Priscilla, who was strikingly beautiful, never expected what would happen that evening, at around ten-thirty, as Vowles completely changed from boyfriend to murderous attacker.

Vowles was hell-bent on killing her but made a very poor job of it. First he took a knife to her throat, and in the dark, she said that she felt something cold on her neck, and then touched her skin to sense blood. As she panicked, Vowles took out a revolver – fired, but failed to do any serious harm with two shots. They struggled, and Priscilla took him on. She managed to extricate herself from his grip and ran off into the night in extreme distress, eventually reaching the house of a Mr Clark, crying for help. She was covered in blood.

The law soon caught up with Vowles. He was found in a field by a Constable Stones, cowering in a field near to Greetland railway station, and he was taken into custody while his sweetheart was in the Halifax Royal Infirmary. Amazingly, she was so slightly injured, in spite of the loss of blood, that she was released and she was taken to the home of Vowles' parents.

Vowles, a moulder at the Perseverance Works of James Lumb in Elland, had failed yet again to kill someone while on the run – this time it was himself. He had fired a shot at the side of his head, caused a severe wound, but was alive. He was bandaged and apprehended. As so often in these cases, the assailant was said locally to be 'a decent young man' and the usual crowd of folk came to stare at the Lumb works, just to be close to the haunt of such a vile character in their midst.

Vowles was taken not far from here, at the railway halt further up from this viaduct in Greetland. The author

The local newspaper actually sent a man to the crime scene, and he wrote about the deserted, lonely corner of a field where the attack took place – at a spot on the point at which Elland, Southowram and Halifax boundaries touch: indeed a perfect place for a murder if the killer wants to be unobserved. The reporter clearly fancied himself as an investigator, as he notes that he saw blood, signs of a violent struggle, and then, rather

This was the lane in Greetland (Nabb End) where Vowles was first tracked.
The author

plangently, he notes the presence of flies, attracted to the spot by the fresh blood.

John Clark, of Park Gate West, was the first to see the unfortunate girl after the crime: he said that he heard no shots or screams, but Priscilla ran straight into his home, without knocking, in a very distressed state, shouting, 'Oh don't let him come in!' She referred to a man down the field who was coming after her. She had run a considerable distance, as Clark's house was more than the length of two fields away from where she was shot. She was unknown to the Clarks, and it must have been an awful shock to them when she charged in, with blood on her head and some also trickling down her neck. Clark saw to her wounds and bandaged her.

Vowles was a popular man, well-known in Siddal. He played football for Salterhebble. The general feeling that 'he was the last person in the world we would have expected to do such a thing' was clearly going around the area at the time. He was 'popular with the youth' of the place. It took some time to track him down: officers went along the fields and the canal bank by Exley. He was found at about five in the morning.

As to the beautiful and distraught Priscilla Milnes, after medical examination, first by Dr Topham and then at the Infirmary, she proved to have several cuts , and a bullet had grazed her head. There had been profuse bleeding, but nothing arterial. She stayed at her sweetheart's house that night, and his mother was bothered and questioned by over-zealous journalists. They reported that she was in tears and in no mood to talk. Amazingly, the young woman at the centre of the affair was detained in hospital only twenty minutes. The mother was caring for someone who, by all accounts, should have been found dead in that field in the early hours.

On 20 September at the Halifax West Riding Court, the magistrates, Aspinall and Robertshaw, must have been taken aback by the sight of young Vowles, heavily bandaged and obviously in considerable pain, lying rather than sitting on the bench as he faced them. When his name had been called, he had been unable to stand up without help from the ushers.

Unbelievably, the cause of the attack had been an argument over a particular football match: they had gone earlier in the day to Salterhebble, and then homewards, to walk in Parklane, and on into the fields. The dispute arose, and Vowles first struck with the knife, then lit a match to see her throat before trying a second time to kill her with the knife. He only succeeded in stabbing her hand. Then the gun was used, and he threw her down to the ground, her face down, before

The area of Salterhebble not far from the attack on Priscilla Milnes. The author

discharging the gun. The first shot missed and the second skimmed her scalp. Priscilla was plucky enough to grab hold of his gun and run into the dark. She lost a broach and her spectacles in the fight.

All the man could do was call after her 'I'm going to go to the end...' and indeed he tried to shoot himself dead. The wound was in his temple but he survived. At the trial, he was not well enough to be fully articulate and said, as he was attended once again for his illness, 'I want to get better and then I can speak.' He was remanded in care for medical treatment before the case could continue.

Once more, there is another story to be told about this crazed attack. If the cause really was so trivial, then why had he taken Priscilla Milnes into that dark and lonely spot – a place for a lover's tryst – with the intention of making it her last place on earth? Why had he taken her there with a knife and a revolver on his person if he had no intent to do her serious harm, or even an intent to end her life? The final explanation was indeed attempted murder. He had wanted her out of the way so that he was free for other liaisons, and the girl had proved not only very spirited, but in fact a formidable opponent.

The family of John Clark must have been more terrified than she, when Priscilla burst into their home on that fateful night, a gun in her hand and blood pouring from her head. It was, after all, in a deserted spot, close to Southowram and in what was then one of the most rural areas of the parish, and indeed was a noted place for that recreational walking and fresh air that the Victorians valued so highly. But a late-night walk taken by two lovers would never have suggested such a savage attack and it was a miracle the poor young woman survived to tell the tale.

As for Salterhebble FC, they lost one of their star players by all accounts, but would they have wanted such an unbalanced and unpredictable character among them?

CHAPTER 34

Knives Out on Christmas Eve
1908

The relationship between Ernest Hutchinson and Hannah Whiteley was stormy, to say the least. For some time before things came to a head and a murder was committed, Ernest had suspected that his young wife, aged twenty four, was earning extra money by entertaining 'gentlemen callers.' They had had several noisy rows over this, and their life had been quite violent.

They had first met in 1907 and they began living together eventually some time in the following year. As early as November in 1907, he had hit Hannah savagely as a result of his suspicions about her prostitution. Things were so bad on that occasion that he had actually been arrested and summoned for obscene language. As time went on, things were made worse, so he claimed, by Hannah's alcohol problem.

This antagonism led to a terrible and tragic outcome on Christmas Eve, 1908, when, late in the evening, neighbours of the couple in Great Albion Street, Halifax, knew that there was something horrific happening in their street.

Hannah had a daughter, Eveline, and people could see the little girl at the window. She was very upset, and clearly weeping and sobbing. Eventually, a certain Tom Greevy scrambled up to open a window. This was prompted by the sight of blood oozing out from under the front door of the house. Greevy forced his way in, and inside he found a dreadful scene: Hannah was dead, lying in blood near the door, and Ernest was in a state of shock, lying on the stairs with a wound in his throat.

As the police began to investigate, it was established that Hannah had been viciously attacked, suffering multiple stab-wounds to the breast and the neck. In contrast, Ernest was not

Great Albion Street, where Greevy murdered Hannah in 1908, on Christmas Eve.
The author

seriously hurt, despite the wound made by a razor. Later, he was treated in hospital and soon released. Questions needed to be asked about that night, and Ernest had a convoluted story to tell.

Ernest had been drinking heavily on that Christmas Eve at the *Star Hotel*, and he had even been joining in the festivities with some local carol singers. The scene did not seem to have a foreboding of evil, but when he returned home he said that he saw a man coming from his home, and that on going inside, he saw money on a plant stand. A row began, as many times before this. But this time, although Hutchinson claimed that Hannah drew a razor on him in anger, he 'happened to have a knife nearby' and attacked her. He must have struck in a wild frenzy to inflict so many severe wounds.

It did not take long for the jury to decide he was guilty of murder, but they did give a strong recommendation for leniency, as he was only twenty-four. Feelings were so strong in this regard that 8,500 signatures in support of leniency were collected. But it did him no good. Henry Pierrepoint hanged Ernest Hutchinson on 2 March, 1909.

The Star, *where Greevy had been drinking.* The author

CHAPTER 35

Strange Death of a Widow
1909

Hannah Binks, of Ashley Cottages, Southowram, was over eighty years old when she was found dead in her home one morning. She was very badly bruised in several places, and the room was in a complete mess, as if someone had ransacked the place and attacked her, perhaps looking for whatever money or goods she had worth the taking. Of course, she was in a vulnerable state, open as an easy target for violent and desperate people who wanted to exploit a chance of quick gain.

Hannah had lost her husband, Joseph, several years before, and had been an active and independent woman for a long

Opposite the Woolshops, a distant view of the hilly Southowram, much more isolated in 1900. The author

time before heart disease slowed her down. But she was well looked after by neighbours; one of them kept a key and was supposedly looking after her welfare. Such does seem to be the case, on the surface, but questions remain. Why were the bruises made at different times, and in places that suggest she had several falls – not simply one night in which she fell and then was discovered the next morning.

There are questions about the case that do not make the verdict of accidental death quite as clear-cut as is apparent from the bare newspaper report. Mr Ryder, a neighbour, gave witness that he found the body. Mrs Sarah Sutcliffe, who had the key, said that she saw Hannah making tea at about half past five on the evening before she was found dead. Then, as Mrs Sutcliffe returned home later, Hannah's house was in darkness and it was assumed that the old lady had gone to bed. But was there an intruder? She would be an easy victim.

There was certainly a radical upset in her home, all the furniture in a mess and all chairs turned over. If she had fallen, if had been more like a mini-maelstrom than a tumble across a table and chairs. Hannah had been seen out and had been noted as feeble. One man had written a note to the relieving officer for the area, suggesting that she be supervised in some way. Common knowledge was that she was very vulnerable.

At this point, it seems fairly straightforward. But then there is the knife. A knife had been seen in her room: it was noted as being at the bottom of her bed by Mr Ryder one day. Mrs Sutcliffe saw this, too, and said that she thought it had been knocked off a shelf or off the table. What was never asked or pressed is why? Why would there be a knife there at all? If there had been an intruder who subsequently attacked Hannah Binks, then there was a weapon to hand for them to use.

She had had a spell in hospital a year before this event, and a 'lady doctor' giving evidence says that Hannah was in a bad way, with arterial deterioration. But again, a woman so frail would hardly have wrecked a room in falling over. When bruises had been noted on her on previous occasions, she had replied that she had fallen.

What really went on during that night of 21 September, will never be known. The simple and accepted answer may well be the truth, but there are doubts, and it was indeed a remarkable affair, asking more questions than were answered at the inquest. When chairs had been seen overturned on previous occasions, Hannah had answered that she had 'been tidying up a bit.' It may even be the case that she was losing her mind and had experienced some kind of apoplexy. The facts are shrouded in the mists of time, like so many distant events in lonely places.

CHAPTER 36

Found with her Throat Cut
1909

Livingstone Twaite, of Shroggs Road, liked to keep poultry and enjoy some peace and quiet. But that was when he wasn't working, and when he was working he had money for drink. That was his downfall. On 21 October, 1909, when full of drink, he attacked the woman he was living with, Beatrice Smith, to the neighbours, and cut her throat.

Thwaite was a tempestuous character, unbalanced in the extreme. He had already left his wife to live with Beatrice. To complicate things further, she was really Beatrice Cooke, the wife of a boatman. Her partner severed her jugular and left her bleeding to death on the road. They had gone for a walk together in Birks Wood. Her body was found near to Royston Mill, after Thwaite had walked into the police station in Harison Road and confessed to the crime.

Thwaite had been living with his wife in Fairfield Terrace for around seven months; they had no children. He was well known in the area for being rowdy and offensive, and his rows with his new wife were usually overheard by others in the street. On four or five occasions when they had quarrelled, his wife had left him to go and stay with her mother. Again, neighbours knew of his tendency to drink heavily and lose control.

Thwaite had attacked Beatrice most viciously on their walk, and he had rolled the body down a slope by a tip, before cutting her throat, as there were no signs of any struggle on the road above. But there was a deep gash in her throat; he had meant to finish her, for sure. At the top of the slope, police found her 'Merry Widow' style hat, trimmed with feathers and roses, a hat-pin and brooch. The slope was thirty feet deep.

Two sergeants, Ramsden and Whitaker, searched Thwaites' home but found no knife. They found a puppy, a bed recently

Shroggs Road today, where Livingston lived, and close to Birks Wood, where he and Beatrice walked. The author

slept in, and on the table a long, signed confession from the young man who worked as a painter and paper-hanger at Robinson's. A customer summed up the problem: 'a nice young man you couldn't wish to meet, except when he's in his drink ... when he's a regular luney'

Neighbours heard him shouting in his drunken state, 'The only woman I have loved and I've murdered her.. come and look and I'll show you where I have put her... I'm going to give myself up...' Some were aroused from sleep, but on seeing him, they put it down to his usual inebriated ravings and left him to wander around the streets. He was well-known in the town, having lived in Pellon Lane, and also being a soldier, leaving the service just before the Boer War. But he had been noticed causing a public nuisance well before this awful crime. On one occasion he had been railing at folk and fell over a wall, with a deep drop at the other side. People expected his body to be found at the bottom of the Corporation quarry at Stannary, but he was up and about again soon after. He had fallen onto a ledge just eight feet below and been rescued, so that he could continue his roistering, swaggering life in the pubs, where he was renowned as a top darts player.

He and his wife were just twenty seven; she talked of buying him pigeons and fowl to occupy his time when unemployed, but pointed out that he had always been in the habit of beating her when in his drink. She spoke of enduring five years of misery since they married. Once he chased her out of the house, beating and haranging her, then catching up with her and dragging her back inside. But recently he had started carrying a knife, and she had been living in fear for her own life. Then, after Beatrice's death and her husband under arrest, she felt a mixture of fear and relief. She commented afterwards that she thought he had really wanted to kill her, not his new partner.

Poor Beatrice White/Cooke had indeed been living something of the lifestyle of the glamorous 'Merry Widow' as suggested by her fashion sense and love of the life of excitement; maybe she wanted to live fast and loose, but it had its awful penalties and risks. She was enmeshed with the worst kind of man.

In the dock before the presiding magistrate, Alderman Wallace, Thwaite was at first fretful and shrinking down, almost cowering. After he was ordered to stand up straight, he simply listened to his remand being issued. He had to listen coldly, now his sober self, to the account of the woman he loved (as he claimed) being found in a tip with a gashed throat, and being taken to the mortuary. He was responsible: no-one else. So ended the story of a man utterly possessed by alcohol, his state totally transformed like Jekyll and Hyde. The story reinforces a trend observed in the study of violent crime against the person in the poorer areas of West Riding towns, and this is seen very clearly in Halifax: the factor of ignorance about the nature and effects of alcohol. So many criminals must have been similar to Livingstone Thwaite, and while this does not exonerate him, it does again highlight the awful condition of those criminals who may well have had severe medical conditions and for whom heavy drinking was a sure recipe for disaster – if not for them, then for their victims.

CHAPTER 37

The Last Straw
1919

Arthur Medd had a high tolerance level; by today's standards he would have been considered depressed, and most likely suffering from work-related stress. But the fact is that on a winter's night he took his own life, simply launching himself into the canal in a spot just a short way out of Sowerby Bridge. The reasons why are maybe more commonly understood now than in 1919. He was only twenty-six and comfortably off, as they say in Yorkshire.

It had a lot to do with the war; he had lost his only brother, and his mother had died of what seems like the 'flu. In short, he was alone. Like modern stories in which some unfortunate old person is found dead in a soulless flat in some inner city slum, Medd's is a tale of a man quietly going under, with nothing left to live for. He was thought to be the quiet man in the corner at work, where he was an accounts clerk. People thought he had nothing to talk about but birds and flowers, as these were his one interest. He would walk for hours up above Mytholmroyd or Warley, walking from King Cross, where he lived.

There was no note. He was found by passers-by, who said that they had seen him in that area on previous occasions. The description of him is that he was tall and thin, and spoke as if he could have been someone 'of substantial position', a Mrs Widdop, who spoke to him at more than one time, said. But the presiding magistrate, after listening to the medical evidence, had no doubt that the poor man had not been attacked, and that his mortal injuries were caused by drowning and that there were no signs of any previous injury or assault.

A Mr Templeman who worked with him for many years, said that the death of Medd's brother had been like losing a piece of himself. He had moped and fretted, and life seemed to lose

Medd's body was found close to this spot leading down to Sowerby Bridge.
The author

all its purpose. In his house were found books on field birds and works of botany; he had pressed wild flowers into one of his small pocket-books.

Reading the accounts of Medd by neighbours and workmates, one is reminded of Thoreau's famous remark that most men live lives of quiet desperation. This definitely applies to this poor *auto da fe*. He was the type of man who would have probably written a reflective journal of some kind, so internalised was his life. But there was nothing found. He had lived a life of simplicity, with, as one witness commented, 'a front room free from dust, as if a cleaner had been busy at work every day to keep it so...' But on that apparently uncommonly mild November night, he chose to end his life as simply as he had lived it.

The death of his brother just fifteen months before was most likely the last straw for the poor man. He apparently liked walking alone into the country, and sometimes at night; he was a great reader and aspired to 'culture' and his story is an extreme version of so many who were trapped in the loneliness of that era, when cities and how we live in them were changing our sense of who we are.

CHAPTER 38

The Crib Lane Murder
1926

I n this case there is a photograph that tells a story of its own, the images making up the picture raising more questions than are answered. The two smartly-dressed men are looking through the window of a house in Crib Lane, in July, 1926. To locals, it has become a macabre scene, with a brutal murder of a pregnant woman at the centre of it.

On the photograph, someone has placed an 'X' in the road, and that is where William Cornelius Jones, aged twenty-two, shot his wife in cold blood, and in a public place. Surely the children gathered outside represent the usual crowd of morbidly

Crib Lane, Halifax. X marks the spot where Jones shot Winnitred. Today, it is a grassed area near Dean Clough parking. Evening Courier

curious people, and the men are most likely two reporters. It was indeed a sensational, inexplicable act of barbarity.

William Jones was a labourer, but he was also a member of the Territorial Army. On the day he killed Winnifred in Crib Street, he had been going with some fellow soldiers to a parade in Bradshaw, when he met his estranged wife on his way to catch a tram in Corporation Street. They appear to have ignored each other's presence, but the territorials with the killer were asked to go on and told that William would meet them later on. It was a fatal meeting: the young man had collected a gun at the Halifax Drill Hall for use in the parade, of course. But he had other thoughts.

He loaded the rifle and shot Winnifred as she stood in the street. The girl was only two weeks away from giving birth to their child; she was rushed to the Royal Halifax Infirmary, but was dead on arrival. People heard Jones say, as he stood and watched her dying in front of him, 'I have done it. You have no need to be frightened. I shan't run away.' This is surely one of the most crass and meaningless farewells given to someone fighting for their last breath. But there was no drama, no attempt to run or to come up with a story of any kind to escape the inevitable sentence of death. There he stood, in a street in a crowded part of working class Halifax where several streets cover the gradual slope down to Dean Clough Mills, and waited for arrest. It must have been with a sense of awe and uneasiness that the crowd gathered to watch the scene as the young man simply did the terrible act and then waited for justice.

William Jones was hanged in Armley Jail, Leeds, in January 1927. As has been pointed out by other writers, there is the name 'A.Jones. Horse Collar Maker' written on the lintel of the house next to the Crib Lane home of the Jones's, and it may be that there is some family connection. We will never know, just as the bizarre workings of this killer's mind will always be a mystery. His friends waited in vain for the chance to march with him in the ranks of the West Riding Territorial Regiment. He was doing what he had been trained to do, in a way, but why he fired the shot is a mystery.

But there had certainly been no mystery: Ada Greenwood stated that she had clearly seen the man raise the rifle, ready to take aim and another person had seen him load the gun.

CHAPTER 39

The Bowling Club Sensation
1927

On the evening of 9 March, 1927, attractive young wife, Ruth Scholefield had left home to enjoy herself at a concert being given at the Gibbet Street Institution. She never came home, and her husband, John, read a description of a woman found, along with a man, who had died from gas poisoning.

Ruth and the man, a greenkeeper at the Stafford Bowling Club, had been found by the club stewardess who was checking the working of some gas fires. On the floor she found the bodies: Ruth, a mother-of-two, and Clement Taylor, aged forty-seven, in the boiler house. There was a scandal around these deaths, and as the *Courier* reported, one of Ruth's children grew up with the belief that her mother had been murdered.

Ruth Swift had come to the area around 1901, from St Helen's, and her parents died in the nineteen thirties, and are buried in Sowerby Bridge. In 1919, she married John Edward Scholefield, a textile worker, and they settled near Pellon Lane, in West Mount Street. They had two children, Gordon and Irene, and there is a photograph of Ruth with her children still surviving. She was indeed an attractive woman; the police description makes it clear that she dressed well, and the petite five feet four inch tall woman was wearing colourful and classy clothes on the day of her death, including a fawn telemac raincoat and a green silk blouse.

At the inquest, John Scholefield was asked if Ruth was in the habit of going out alone, and John replied that she did, and that most often these trips were to visit her mother in Norland, and he had believed her. But things were not quite so simple, and he was surely duped. Many people had seen Ruth out and about with Clement Taylor; in fact one woman, a Maud Day, had actually reported seeing the couple in Westgate fisheries

Stafford street today, south of the parkland leading up to Skircoat and beyond.
The author

on that night when they had died. Mrs Day said that they had asked her to join them for a drink, and that they had been drinking already when she met them. If they should have had something to hide, it didn't seem like it on this evidence. They were flaunting the affair.

From there they had gone to the clubhouse, and it seems that they were by the boiler for warmth. The inquest found no evidence of foul play and it seems that they died from carbon monoxide poisoning. Everything points to a boiler fault, and when the heat was turned down, they had fallen asleep and the leak had killed them, as their corpses were pink, and were clearly dead due to that effect.

The sad turn in the Scholefield story comes when we learn that John Scholefield would no longer take any responsibility for caring for his children, and they were sent to children's homes. Irene died in 1971 in Ormskirk, after marrying a man there; but Gordon survives. Now a grandchild, Kathleen Spencer, is looking for Ruth's grave; there had been a belief in the family, perpetuated by Irene, that their mother had been murdered.

Ruth Scholefield and her children. The picture as taken two years before the 'death by gassing' story made the news. The author

That is, of course, now resolved; but the story of Ruth and Clement has all the traits of an affair that met with a tragic end, and of a lingering bitterness in the aftertaste of such an unpleasant and fateful liaison. But they took risks, and seemed to almost enjoy that public visibility of their closeness; yet their deaths were ironically 'secret' and had to be discovered by accident and with a real sense of shock.

CHAPTER 40

Abandoned Infants
1928

On 3 November in this year, Walter Turner crossed Whitegate Bridge at about four-thirty when he noticed a woman pointing to a parcel on the canal bank. Walter found a rake somewhere and managed to haul in the package. As he opened it, the tiny body of a child emerged. He told police that he thought it had not been there long. But this was the first of two infants' corpses found within two days in Halifax. This was Siddal: the second was at King Cross.

Constable Robinson said, at the inquest, that he had discussed with Inspector Darby the evidence of a broken branch nearby, and that this was clearly a sign of where the person bringing the child had gone down to the water's edge. The baby was wrapped in very clean brown paper and

Willowfield today, close to where one of the dead infants was found. The author

amazingly, some of the paper was not at all wet. The body was that of a female child, but it was not identifiable.

The post-mortem noted that the child was fully developed and well nourished; it had been there for two or three days. She had not been washed, and death was due to what a medical professional called 'inattention at birth'. It was not uncommon at that time, with such ignorance about hygiene and diet rife in poorly-educated working people's lives. The awesome legal term of 'no separate existence' was used.

But the second child found presented a different scenario. This one was found by a Roy Pedley of Browfoot Gate, who was searching hedges and ditches for clothes for his Guy when he noticed a macintosh under a stone wall. This was in willow field, near to Burnley Road. The little body was only a yard or so from the path where people walked along the road edge. Pedley looked closer and saw that the item was a rubber-lined lady's mac. But far more disturbing for the boy was the sight of blood on the brown paper wrapped around the badly decomposed corpse.

Siddal WMC. *Only yards from this corner, a dead child was found.* The author

Pedley ran to fetch a policeman from King Cross, and that officer, on closer inspection of the package, was unable to say for sure whether the child was male of female, it was in such a degenerated state. Later, on medical inspection, Dr Lindsay Clark said that it was female, weighing seven pounds and six ounces, and being about twenty-two inches in height and fully developed. But this was more sinister, as it had been dead for eight to ten days, but had been maltreated and most likely killed – of course, as the phrase goes, 'by person or persons unknown', and a murder verdict for sure.

The fact that such abandoned corpses of infants had always been a common occurrence never makes them less distressing of course, and the stories told are always of how these tragic deaths figured so prominently in a normal day; the fact that the second was found by a young boy is all the more emotive, and the matter-of-fact details reduce the murder almost to a condition of desperate actions by people with huge moral and financial pressures upon them to survive, or stories untold, about young people with enormous problems and totally unable to cope in a world without a system of social support.

CHAPTER 41

A Suicide Pact
1930

Narratives of 'foul deeds' do not come very often as profoundly tragic and wasteful as what seemed at first a story of dual suicide: and that is even more touching when there is a muddle in the midst of it all – a very human muddle from a complicated life. But there was also murder, and what is for sure is that there was deep, unremitting melancholy in the tale of Albert Allen, aged thirty, and Phyllis Crummy, aged twenty-five.

Mytholmroyd today, seen from the bridge just half a mile from Stocks Road.
The author

Allen was a coal merchant from Stocks Yard, Mytholmroyd, and at the end of this awful story he was indicted for the murder of the woman he loved. Phyllis was from Ovenden, and she had a child of her own. Allen had two children also, when they first formed a relationship. But their liaison ended with them being found lying on an old mattress in a flat in London, before a gas fire. They were found by the proprietor, and there was a suicide note which read (from Allen) addressed to his mother:

> *I have no regrets except I am leaving you and Jeff behind. I am going with the girl I love and who loves me to the bitter end. Tell the relatives I am not insane, but this is the best for me.*

Allen had been in the air force, but then came back home to his job as a coal merchant, and his father said he was 'a good son'. But Allen didn't die. He said in court that he and Phyllis had gone for a week together in London, but when he had wanted to return north, and she hadn't. She wanted to take

Stocks Road leading to Stocks Yard (now an ice-cream factory) where Albert Allen lived. The author

morphia, he said. Allen expressed her mood as 'fanatical' and when they finally did arrange things so they could exit, she disconnected the gas stove and lay down, sucking a pipe. Allen said he had no idea what to do in that situation, and insisted that he had pulled her away three times. Finally, giving up on the whole thing, he testified that 'seeing the whole thing so serious I thought I would do the same.'

Of course, now the questions start. If he saw such a serious situation, beyond his remedy, why did he not call for help? The court concluded that there was no agreement to die together. What was sure is that when Allen had left, he had done so quickly, and his father said that Allen and Phyllis had been discussing living together for some time before this happened. Allen had gone south and left a note for his father, saying it was no use trying to follow him..

Phyllis's state of mind is more complex: her husband, Clement Crummy of Sheffield, had been sending her a regular weekly sum of one pound, and they had recently been discussing living together again, and trying to fix up a time to meet and talk.

It all starts to make sense and appears to have two versions: one is a desperately suicidal young woman, drifting away from any stable life and relationship, heading for a distant spot where she could end it all, and seemingly with a man of similar intentions. But then, he cannot go through with it, panics and bungles everything, himself surviving. The other version is that he wants rid of her and fakes the suicide, actually murdering her by surviving the pact.

The trial led to neither interpretation, and that is for the simple reason that English law at this time considered any survivor of a suicide pact to be guilty of murder. It seems completely heartless and extreme through modern eyes. Hence one of the most heart-rending stories of deaths in Halifax, or involving Halifax people.

CHAPTER 42

The Missionary Murder
1930

Edith Nettleton was surely one of Halifax's most notable and arguably heroic figures, going from employment at the Dean Clough Mills, study in Highbury, and then to missionary work in China. But in 1930, while working in Fuhkein, she was shot dead by bandits, along with her friend, Eleanor Harrison, of Kidderminster. The story was news on a grand scale in the press of that year, and her life-story makes for an exciting read.

Edith was born in Halifax, the daughter of Arthur Nettleton and his wife (Christian name unknown). Her mother was still alive and living in Gladstone Road when news of Edith's death

Edith Nettleton, who once worked at Dean Clough, but was killed by bandits in China. Author's collection

CONSUL GIVEN AUTHORITY TO PAY RANSOM.

The Rev. W. W. Cash, general secretary of the Church Missionary Society, told a reporter in London, to-day:

"Miss Harrison and Miss Nettleton were captured by bandits, when, acting under Consul's orders, they were going down river from their station at Chungan to Foochow.

"The bandits boarded the steamer and took them off, and since then unremitting efforts for their release have been made by the British Consul, C.M.S. missionaries, and the Chinese Church.

"Both the Consul and the secretary of the C.M.S. in Foochow were given an entirely free hand to pay the ransom, if necessary, in order to secure the release of the ladies.

"Up to this week, it was hoped that these efforts would be successful. The news received this morning has, therefore, come as a great blow to the Society, and will cause profound sorrow to all who knew the two ladies and

MISS EDITH NETTLETON.

They are being kept to attend to the wounded, when the Communists suffered a heavy defeat in their attack on Caungan City and I gather they are not being

Family Without News.

Miss Nettleton's Career in the Mission Field.

Seen by our representative this morning, one of Miss Nettleton's brothers stated that the family had not received any intimation of the shooting of the two lady missionaries. A few weeks ago a letter was received from the London Missionary Society stating that there was a rumour in China that Miss Nettleton had died, but there had been no confirmation of it.

The family and Miss Nettleton's many friends in Halifax are naturally distressed at to-day's news, and indeed the whole country will be shocked that such a tragedy should be possible in the 20th century.

HER EARLY AMBITION.

Miss Nettleton was well known in Halifax, being an active church worker prior to deciding upon a career of useful service on the mission field. She was a daughter of the late Mr. Arthur and Mrs. Nettleton, the latter of whom, now

Gladstone Road today: this is where the Nettletons lived. The author

reached home. The missionary had been in China for many years, and had lived a dangerous life, often being on river-boats and being under fire from political factions. The natives had at first been friendly, but with political change came new threats to their safety; Edith and Eleanor were the only Europeans for hundreds of miles in their area of missionary work.

The news of the shooting came in a simple message by telegram from the Church Missionary Society: 'Nettleton and Harrison shot: Consul and Sills returning Foochow'; Sills was the Reverend Alfred Sills, who had been trying in vain, through the British Consulate, to bring about the women's release. Four months earlier, the bandits had asked for the sum of £5,000 for the release of their hostages, and this never materialised. They sent a package to Peking containing one of Miss Nettleton's fingers, to show that they were in earnest.

Edith had been home to Halifax just a year before her murder, at home on furlough, attending several meetings on behalf of the missions. She was, ironically, about to be moved to a safer area. But in her time in that region, she had always done everything asked of her, and carried on in spite of danger

Gibbet Street today, the street where Edith went to school and church. The author

and the increasing presence of troops in the area around her base. In the previous six years, a total of thirty- three missionaries had been shot, and another eighty- nine held to ransom.

The Consul, Mr Martin, had been in action in the province of Fuhkien for some time, moving missionaries to safer places, and he had transferred all but the two ladies; and after that, learning of their capture, he managed to get soldiers sent after them to try to counteract the threat. But all was to no avail. Edith, aged forty-nine, and Eleanor, aged sixty-three, were captured in Chunghai, near Fuhkien, by the forces of Luh Sing-Pang, a rebel leader. He at first treated them well, but things deteriorated. There was no hope, and eventually, the fateful message came through. Her brother at home in Halifax, had recently said that he had heard nothing definite, and then the whole town was shocked as the terrible news came through.

Edith Nettleton had died nobly; she had been engaged in trying to help the wounded involved in the civil war just shortly before being taken; surely, here was the murder of a local hero. The wilds of South China, many said at the time, was 'no place for a woman': well, it was no place for anyone except the brave and idealistic. Edith was certainly those things, and she made the headlines after her death, despite being a quiet, unassuming worker for her beliefs in her industrious and pious life.

Chapter 43

The Notorious Christie
1943–1951

For the most undesirable of reasons, John Christie is surely the most famous, or infamous murderer associated with Halifax. In the current tourist material 'selling' the area to visitors, he figures alongside Phyllis Bentley and Percy Shaw (the inventor of cats' eyes), and by now, fifty years after his execution for the series of murders of women at 10 Rillington Place, his Halifax connection is alive and well in the media. In the new (2003) part-work, *Real-Life Crimes* (Eaglemoss) he is called 'The Beast of Rillington Place' and the crime historian, Colin Wilson, refers to him as being responsible for 'the greatest murder mystery of all time'.

John Reginald Halliday Christie was born in Black Boy House, Boothtown, Halifax in 1898, and spent the first twenty years of his life there, up to the time of his enlistment to fight in the Great War, in which he was gassed. He was the youngest of four children, with an indulgent mother and a very strict father. Biographical comments note that he was reserved and socially withdrawn. There is an agreement that his fear of women began here; his first sexual experience was so deeply wounding in terms of his sense of personal inadequacy that it confirmed his nick-name as 'Can't Do It Reggie' and 'Johnny No-Dick'amongst his peers at school, as word spread around that he was impotent. This detail was to have a telling effect on the manner of his later murders in London. To make matters worse, his father, who was a carpet-designer – was a rough and capricious man who maltreated and bullied all his family.

In Halifax, it seems certain that one of his first and most powerful memories – that of seeing his grandfather's corpse – was a negative yet formative experience on his psychological traits. He managed to find a job locally, as a postal clerk, but

Boothtown today, close to Bankfield Museum. The author

there were resentments and inadequacies growing in him that the experience of war would certainly do nothing to alleviate.

He was always drawn to power and status, however small, and also drawn to petty theft. The war left him with damaged vocal chords (he was always quietly spoken after this) and also he was blinded for five months. But he came back into society, this time as first a crook and later a special constable, which seems amazing considering the fact that he beat up a prostitute in Halifax and served some short prison sentences. He married Ethel Waddington from Sheffield in 1920; she left him in 1924 but returned when he was in London by 1933. While away from Ethel he had met another woman and this ended after he attacked her with a cricket bat. Life was always going to be hard for her with him; they did not have successful sexual intercourse until two years after their marriage, for instance; and he had a violent streak in him.

But in 1939 he became a war reserve policeman and was living with Ethel at the end of the cul de sac, Rillington Place. This is now no longer in existence; but the spot where he committed at least six murders is now to the west of Ladbroke Grove station at a place called Ruston Close at first, but then demolished, so a street called Bartle Road is apparently the nearest location to the awful den he created where he gassed,

Terraces in Boothtown, typical of what the area would have been like when Christie was brought up here. The author

raped and murdered his victims. The original 10 Rillington Place was a very dull building comprising three flats, and Christie and Ethel lived on the ground floor, having a tiny garden and a wash-house.

He was seen by neighbours as a man who 'knew how to do things', and that included medical knowledge, including a reputed ability to carry out a termination of a pregnancy. But when he first moved into the flat with Ethel, he was obviously conscious of the fact that he had a record, and would want to be seen as an honest citizen and a helpful man in the close community.

When new tenants, Timothy and the pregnant Beryl Evans moved in as neighbours in 1948, after Christie had done his first murders, it seems that Christie killed the mother and child and let Timothy take the rap, being hanged for their murder. There is doubt, however, and much of it concerns the fact that Timothy went to a police station in Wales in 1949 to confess that he had 'disposed of the body' of his wife. But finally, after killing three prostitutes as well as other visitors to his lair, he strangled Ethel on 14 December 1950 and buried her under the floorboards. But things went from bad to worse in his career generally; leaving the police, he worked for a company called Ultra Radio and here he lured Muriel Eady to come in, on the pretext of having a cure for her catarrh.

He was now an expert in his own peculiar and ritualistic method of killing: using a rubber pipe attached to a gas source and inserting this under a cloth as the victim thought she was inhaling something healthy. He also plied them with drink.

The most unpleasant and barbaric aspect of Christie's murderous habits was that he was a necrophile, as forensic evidence has shown, based on semen found in the bodies of victims and semen on his shoes. He would gas, rape and then stash the bodies in a cupboard which was later closed in and wall-papered, leaving a permanently unpleasant smell in the place, of course. The room and cupboards were maintained at a high temperature, so the bodies, when eventually found, were of a pinkish colour and the semen was easily assessed in terms of the physiology of the spermatozoa.

So the method went on, until the last killing, of Hectorina Maclennan in 1953. He even gave her boyfriend tea, after killing her and stacking her in the closet. The nasty smell the man commented on was his girlfriend's rotting corpse. Christie was found soon after this, wandering aimlessly around, by a constable, who asked if he was John Christie. He went quietly, and was executed not very long after the last murder, on 15 July 1953.

One of the major mysteries of this case is why the police, when they first came to look at the flat and a second time when they were supposed to search it more thoroughly, did they not look in the wash-house? The law also believed Christie's story that he was unable to help Timothy get rid of Mrs Evans's body because he was suffering from fibrosis and so could do no heavy lifting. The bodies were found only on the third police visit. All this is very similar to the questions asked of the police during the Sutcliffe investigations, when he was several times in their hands and was not suspected.

The media in Halifax, of course, gave the trial and the execution lead stories, and retold the tale of the Calderdale connection. The images reproduced of him show a thin, gaunt figure, with a haunted look: underfed and almost cadaverous in fact. There is the usual bathos of the 'ordinary' little man of the photograph being totally at odds with the heartless killer, as in the picture of him standing with his dog. The dog sniffs at a flower as Christie stands, unmoved, wearing his smart suit, the epitome of the respectable citizen. But as Colin Wilson comments, the best accurate description of this man is of an 'older' type of killer: 'the conventional little man with a violent sexual appetite that drives him to rape in much the same furtive spirit as a poacher stealing game.' In spite of this, it has to be said that Christie's rituals and perversions colour him with a profoundly sick psychosis which led him to perpetrate a peculiar variety of evil and a sexual deviancy met with only in a certain pattern of serial murder, with related mental illness.

It would seem to be a story that Christie's place of birth and early life would want to forget, but murder is always news and scandal; in the case of the 'Beast of Rillington Place' he is of the same high status in the annals of murder as The Boston Strangler or Haigh of the acid bath, and his notoriety will always have that Halifax dimension, like it or not.

CHAPTER 44

Murdered in Bed
1944

Police were scouting the Halifax road in Queensbury in June, 1944, looking for two soldiers, both on the run and very likely the murderers of a lonely widow who kept the *Nag's Head* at Clayton. They were never traced, and probably disappeared back into the war, or maybe went underground and vanished – the latter being the more likely explanation as they were known. One was known and the other not, so the mystery thickens. One physical description was that the unknown one was about thirty years of age, about five feet eight inches tall and of moderate build; his badge was of the Seaforth Highlanders. It was all so blatant and crass, that the uniforms may even have been false, according to one commentator.

The other was Ltn Corporal Arthur Thompson of the General Service Corps. He had been absent without leave since three days before this murder. He was twenty-four, of a sallow complexion and heavily built. He was in battle dress, with a notable minor feature of a bakelite helmet.

They (or other persons unknown) had committed a brutal killing that night. What had happened was that Jane Coulson, a widow, was found strangled in her bed, a lisle stocking around her neck. She was sixty-nine and lived alone, except for her much-loved pet dog, a fox terrier bitch. A friend, Mrs Somerfield, said that the victim was 'beginning to feel her loneliness'. Jane had been strict on security as she was living alone: she had strong bolts on the back door, including one which needed hammering into position. But it was not enough to stop the killer or killers gaining access through a kitchen window.

The unknown soldier had been seen only 400 yards from the public house, on the Halifax side of the road. There had been quite a hoard of diamonds taken from Mrs Coulson, too, including two 18-carat dress rings. Police also found an empty cotton bag, and this was found to be the bag she kept under her pillow at night, with the keys to her jewellery-boxes in it. Everything begins to shape up into a scenario of a determined robbery, burglary and eventual murder of a defenceless old lady. It even looks as though the men took the bag of takings, as people knew what this looked like, and it was nowhere on the premises when the police made an extensive search.

The crime was perhaps part of a spree the two men enjoyed while they were drifting across the north, as a taxi-driver in the vicinity had also been killed, just a fortnight before – a Harry Graham of Bradford, murdered in his cab. It seems as though they spent some time at the *Commercial Inn* (once a coaching house) near North Bridge. Could it be that the two desperate men were on the run, maybe even, in one case, in disguise as a soldier? Certainly he was not found, and may have been very clever in this respect. But for some cash and a few gems, Jane Coulson had been heartlessly killed in her bed.

Were the story pure fiction, it would be simple to imagine a scenario in which two rash adventurers on the run entertain and amuse a lonely woman, someone in need of a good time; but then the situation tipped over from good company and drink to violence, and the men perhaps had a carefully planned strategy to extract what they could from the victim.

Once the Commercial, *this is where the runaway soldier-killers were seen. It was once a major coachinghouse and the stable yards still survive.* The author

CHAPTER 45

A Killer Camped in the Park
1944

Mervin Clare McEwen was a rogue and an adventurer, thinking himself too clever to be caught for an opportunist murder in Halifax during the Second World War, but he was wrong; a constable found him out and his incognito life was found out. From there it was a short step to the gallows for a callous murder of an old man.

In February, 1943, McEwen went AWOL from his regiment. He was a Canadian, and so would stand out and be noticed in the Halifax area, particularly as he set up camp in a disused army hut on Savile Park. He seems to have had a certain deadly charm and made friends easily; one such acquaintance was eighty-two year old Mark Turner, who lived

Moorfield Street, where McEwen's victim, Turner, lived. The author

in Moorfield Street. In April, Turner had a friendly evening at his house with McEwen and another man named Crabtree. But on that occasion, McEwen went back to his hut.

But the next day, 3 April, a neighbour, Mr Hall, heard loud knocking at Turner's house. But for some hours that day there was no sound heard inside Turner's house, and as he was normally up early and busy, Hall called the police. He was worried as, when he looked into the house, he saw there was something of a mess, and that was unusual.

The body of the old man was found inside, downstairs where he normally slept on a camp-bed. His killer had been very careless: there were fingerprints evident on a whisky bottle and also battledress and badges of McEwen's regiment, the Royal Canadian Corps. Not surprisingly, there was no sign of the soldier in his temporary billet on Savile Park. He had run away to Manchester, and he was about to start a new life with a new identity and a woman called Annie Perfect, with whom he lived as if married. He was now known as James Acton. He must have thought that he had a bolt-hole and was beyond being traced. But he was wrong.

A view of Savile Park, where McEwen camped. Moorfield Street is only thirty yards from the trees. The author

At this point, something happened that reinforces the view that steady, methodical police work pays dividends, and that even the craftiest villains fall foul of their own arrogance. The Canadian dropped his guard and did something so foolish, it seems amazing that he was caught so easily.

A constable arrived at their house, simply making routine enquiries, but when he explained who he was, McEwen produced an identity card with the name 'Mark Turney' on it. The officer was smart and suspicious, so he asked for a signature. He had seen that the letter 'r' had been changed to 't' and there was something amiss. Amazingly, McEwen signed as Mervin Turney. The game was up.

The killer saw that any attempt to lie his way out of this was futile and gave himself up. His story was that he had indeed gone back to the old man's house in Halifax, cooked some food and drunk whisky. In this state, he struck Turner as he woke up, claiming that it was not intentional. His main line of thought was that he was intoxicated and could not have planned murder. He failed, and in forty minutes, the jury had rejected that. He was hanged in Leeds in February.

CHAPTER 46

He Killed on his Wedding Day
1948

Once again, the area of Southowram proves to be vulnerable to enterprising criminals in this story; its geography makes it something of a fastness and a bolt-hole, steep on the slopes between Brighouse and Halifax, close by Siddal, huddled away from the centre of things. The striking thing is that lone criminals, hunting for victims, fall upon such an inaccessible place, and find it convenient.

Arthur Osborne almost behaved as if he wanted to be caught for suspected murder. On September 23 1948, he talked to a neighbour about old Ernest Westwood, of Law Lane, Southowram, and even mentioned that the man would be quite well off. People had seen him loitering around the back of the house. It came as no surprise, then, that he was the prime suspect when Ernest was found severely injured in his bed on the morning of the 24 September, by his good friend and neighbour, Emily Hainsworth.

Osborne had evidently been trying a variety of gambits to ingratiate himself with the older and more vulnerable residents of the village, and he had even left a note for one Edna Green of New Street, near Law Lane, saying that he had missed her but would return to talk to her again.

The story reached the national press and the *News of the World* reported in detail and named Osborne as the man wanted for questioning. Incredibly, not only had he been up north from the home of his fiancée, Dorothy Ball in Chichester; he had been in Halifax attacking the defenceless old man when he should have been getting married to Dorothy.

Everything was planned and arranged for their marriage, and everything was duly cancelled. He went south, apologised, and took lodgings. As the whole world knew about him, and

The steep slopes of Southowram, where Osborne entered and loitered, murder on his mind. The author

the police were watching all his movements, he caught a train north, saying he was going to sort out what was clearly a silly misunderstanding. He was arrested at Sutton and subsequently, his fingerprints were matched to those at Ernest's home. Osborne confessed that he had broken into the house in Law Lane, intending only to steal, but he said that he was disturbed, and had thrown an object at the source of a voice behind him, vainly trying to put forward a self-defence argument.

Osborne appears to have liked loitering around the streets of Southowram, or drinking down at *The Shears*, towards Corporation Street. The fact is that people saw him and recognised him. He was found guilty, and executed on his twenty-eighth birthday, in Leeds.

Osborne's story is typical of the pattern found in the travelling, scheming criminal who preys on the weak and infirm; everything points to him being something of a fatal charmer. It is easy to imagine him talking his way into the trust and confidence of good, ordinary people, and then exploiting

The Shears, Osborne's place where he could steel himself for crime. The author

or robbing them. He was clearly prepared to use any desperate measures to gain from these capers far from home. Putting his wedding second to a murderous attack was his fatal error, but then he was notably a man prone to making disastrous errors in his inept and short life of crime.

CHAPTER 47

Tragedy at Lister Lane
1953

Throughout the day and much of the night on the 13 August, 1953, police were searching the streets around Lister Lane and Gibbet Street, close to the Percival Whitley College and People's Park. They were looking for a missing six-and-a-half-year-old girl called Mary Hackett, who had been missing since noon on that date. Even the dogs had been called out, including a specially effective animal and its trainer, brought in from Wakefield. It was able to follow a trail down as far as the Belle Vue branch of the Halifax Co-operative Society but rain had interfered with progress.

Mary's family had not been in the area for long. They had come over from Limerick, and had only lived in Lister lane

Lister Lane - the building that used to be the place where Hall spent much time. The author

Part of the original PercevalWhitley College, close to where the sandpit was, where Mary used to play. The author

since the previous December. Her father worked with the Parks Department. Little Mary spoke with an Irish accent and had a slight speech impediment. An officer at the time said she was 'rather timid.' The next day, the search widened, and a radio SOS was put out by the Chief Constable of Halifax, broadcast by the BBC.

Mary liked to explore the streets and the grounds of the nearby college. She liked to play in the sandpit in a college annexe. She had only been out for about ten minutes before she was called in for her dinner, but there was no response. The mother said that Mary had wandered off once before, when she was about four years old, and was eventually found two miles from her home. Now, in Halifax, she had been wearing a green dress and blue and white sandals. People knew who they were looking for.

The police were on the right track when they said, on the 13 August, that she may have wandered into some industrial or commercial premises, because, while her mother was shopping in town and her aunt was making food, Mary had met white-haired, forty-eight years-old church caretaker, George Albert Hall. Hall had been a patient at a mental hospital some time before this, at Burley-in-Wharfedale. Now he was caretaker at

The area around Lister Lane and Francis Street, showing the dark, walled streets typical of Hall's haunts. The author

the Congregational Chapel at Lister Lane. Those two sentences echo ironically in the twenty-first century when such things have still a resonance after the panic of the Soham case and the 'vetting' measures of staff in public positions.

The streets around this church, close to what was formerly the Halifax Central Library, were (and are still) bordered by high hedges and walls. There are many corners, turns and places where people may easily disappear from view. The grounds of the church, the college and the library are all near, so there was a wide area to look at, and much ground which is not easily defensible if a threat arises.

Mary found such a dark place. This was the church grounds, and there she met Hall. She knew her way around, of course, and she had told her aunt that she was going to play in the sand just about five minutes before she was told her dinner would be ready. As with so many cases like this, a child can disappear within a very short time. In this case, it was murder. Little Mary was killed after being battered from behind with a blunt instrument, and then Hall had buried her in the corner of the crypt.

The killer would have seen her often at the brick-sided sandpit, which is only fifty yards from the steps leading up to her own door, but equally, next door to the church where he would be loitering, looking for his opportunity to talk, induce her into a quiet spot and ultimately kill her.

As the dog was searching, Hall had cleverly placed two open cans of paint above the flagstones where he had buried Mary's body; he had also covered the corner where this happened with chairs. It was all so close to where her parents were up and about all night long on the 12 August, searching in vain. The public had been given more and more information in the press, even down to the tiny details that she was wearing a tartan hair ribbon and plaits. The *Evening Courier* supplied several pictures to specify the local geography and the girl's haunts such as the sandpit. They were looking in places which Mary knew well – even her school was very near, St Mary's RC School, in Gibbet Street. Anyone knowing the area would realise that the mature vegetation of the nearby park and grounds of Victorian residences would be prime targets for a search.

But all the while her body was within a few hundred yards of them. It all looked as though he had deviously escaped detection and that the body would remain there indefinitely, as bodies are found quite normally in crypts. But he was too clever, and in the course of a conversation, he told a doctor that Mary had died of mortal injuries to the back of her head. At the time he spoke, police had not publicly given details of the cause of little Mary's death. Her body was not discovered until forty days after her disappearance. One can only imagine the agony of that long wait for the parents and relatives.

Hall was arrested and confessed. He was hanged in Leeds in April 1954. His personality and habits fit in quite neatly to the template of this variety of child-murder. This involves a certain psychosis mixing devious and opportunist cunning with profoundly destructive and homicidal tendencies. Given these traits, there could hardly have been a better physical environment for such a killer to thrive as the streets and buildings around Lister Lane.

CHAPTER 48

The Sweetshop Killing
1957

On Whitsun Saturday of 1957, Detective-Superintendent Hannam and Detective-Sergeant Rowe, both of Scotland Yard, were on their way north to Halifax. They had been called in by the Chief Constable of the town very soon after the body of Emily Pye was discovered, brutally murdered, in the house behind her grocer's shop on Gibbet Street. Emily, aged eighty, had been severely bludgeoned to death in what one officer described as a 'rain of blows to the head' by a ruthless killer.

The town end of Gibbet Street is today in the heart of the Asian population's community; there is a mosque quite near to the shop which still stands where Emily's was all those years ago.

The shop at Rhodes Street today, where Emily had her shop, showing the room behind. The author

The streets around are crowded and busy. The thoroughfare of Gibbet Street leads down to the centre of the town and is always noisy. In 1957 it was not so busy, but it is easy to imagine what it was like then, as the red-brick terraces still stand behind the current establishment, and Back Rhodes Street, in which her home stood and where she was killed, is there, unchanged.

It was a Saturday when she died. Police later found out that the shop and house had been locked from around 1.45 pm. Her body was discovered when her relatives, Mr and Mrs Wilson of Northowram, who had come to invite her to spend some of the holiday with her. Doris Wilson was her niece. But they found the premises locked, and through a window, Derek Wilson saw the old lady's body, covered with a rug.

The whole investigation was dramatic and high-profile. The forensic specialists came, including Professor Tryhorn from the Science Laboratory in Harrogate. Crowds gathered to watch as officers stood around talking, or walking through enclosed alleys, before actions were taken. It was a senseless murder, done for a small amount of money taken from the till. It became clear that another, more substantial amount of money was hidden on the premises and had not been found. Superintendent Hannam said he would not have been able to find it. The murder was possibly not done by anyone who knew her, then, and police at the time think that it may have been an opportunity killing by a passing, casual customer.

It was highly unusual for such a high-level officer to be there. Hannam was very highly thought of in the police. He was a smart and dapper man, with a Homburg and a very expensive suit. A picture in the *Courier* shows him almost posing for the camera, looking dignified and impressive. Now forty-seven, he had been a leading figure in many West End cases, knew several languages, and had been on assignments abroad.

The affair reached almost mythic status in the area for some years, as the name 'Emily Pye' as an unsolved murder by an unknown and very violent aggressor resonated through the community. The woman had been such a popular and warm-hearted person, and had lived alone for fifteen years, but before that had had a 'life-long companion' for thirty years, as

The shop, showing the door to the back flat where the intruder entered. The author

long as she had had the business. At one time when she had been ill and had closed the shop when she was in hospital, she had told her niece that she thought a lot of the customers, and ran the shop more for a hobby than anything else. All the more horrible, then, that such a warm-hearted and sociable woman should die in that way.

A photograph taken of Emily Pye when she went to enjoy a Park Ward old folks' treat shows a round-faced, very good-humoured woman smartly dressed and with an open, approachable face. She had been asked about the dangers of living alone in such a vulnerable way, but not shown much concern. Everything about her personality suggests a person who is happy to help others and feel the satisfaction of helping the neighbourhood, knowing her customers and doing what all local shops do: cater for individual needs and order things when in demand.

But considerable force was used to kill her; it has all the hallmarks of a violent robbery, and it never became apparent exactly how and why so much violence was used: whether Emily tried to resist, or possibly whether the assailant used increasing force and brutality when he could not ascertain the existence or whereabouts of more cash or valuables. A quick survey of Back Rhodes Street demonstrates that, if the attacker was shut in with his victim for what could have been a few hours, then it would not have been difficult to be heard through walls, so the murderer may have had to use force to silence the victim rather quickly, particularly if she made a noise or cried for help.

One thing is certain: this was a nasty killing of a well-liked old lady with no defence, and all done for a small sum (exactly how much was never revealed) and the killer is as yet unknown. The possibility of the killer knowing Emily, and thus adding a totally unlikely and contradictory element to the story, is denied by the general standing of the victim in that network of streets. It was a holiday Saturday and a crowd gathered to watch proceedings. It was a time of the week when strangers might have been passing through, perhaps for sporting events. It appears to be likely that a stranger took a chance to grab what was there, and nothing stood in his or her way – not even a weak old lady. The killer also must have grasped very quickly the fact that the housing to the back of the shops along Gibbet Street provided excellent cover and protection for such a vile act to be committed.

The ultimate irony had to be that the plain, low-key and forthright Emily Pye attracted in her death almost a media frenzy of law officers who became virtual celebrities overnight, such was the horrific moral outrage in the town at this crime. Such detail was given about the Holmsian figure of Hannam that we were even told about his son, and the fact that he wore 'designer' clothes. Emily Pye would no doubt have not been impressed.

Such heartless killings of vulnerable old women are definitely a classification of crime, as there are many cases (for instance the murder of Constance Aris in Cheltenham in 1985 which has some similarities to this) but the statistic of most murderers being known by their victims has a powerful application in this case, because when the killer locked himself and Emily in that back room, some time passed, and it seems likely that he or she knew of the existence of the other, unfound stash of money.

Everything about this murder in such an ordinary, peaceful neighbourhood led to that mythology that surrounds any place in which a killer is 'abroad' but never found.

CHAPTER 49

Death in a Playground
1971

Early in the morning of 21 March 1971, a man out walking his dog found the body of a young woman in playing fields near the *Commercial Hotel*. Within a few hours, the whole area would be swarming with police, led by D C S Donald Craig, searching for clues as to what exactly had happened, for a lot had indeed being going on to lead to this violent death. Young Pamela Davis, a WRAF nurse working in Halton, Buckinghamshire, had been viciously attacked and had died due to the act of drowning in her own blood. The bleeding had come from her fractured skull.

When the dog-walker roused a young man at a nearby house a chain of circumstances began, all emanating from the fact that there are several pubs nearby, and police later learned from Pamela's parents that she had been expected home the night before, after having a night out with her friend, Kathleen. She never came home, and Kathleen said that Pamela left her at the pub at ten-thirty. This enabled police to put a time to the murder, as the doctor noted that she had been killed between ten and eleven the previous night.

What was markedly sickening about this murder was that young Pamela had fought hard for her life and was not only bruised and cut, but bitten as well, and medical examination confirmed that the marks were made by a human. A large stone had been used to fracture her skull, and although she had not been raped, there appeared to have been a sexual motivation for the attack. Clothes were scattered across the area; some were found under a rock. So vigorous had the fight been that her bra was torn, as were most of her clothes. A young man living nearby said he had heard a scream but had thought that to be nothing unusual as young couples were often 'larking about' in that recreation area of a Saturday

The building that was the Commercial, *where Ainley had been seen drinking on the night of the killing.* The author

night. But searches and local enquiries were thorough; the first breakthrough came when a couple were interviewed and talked about seeing a young man leave the scene that night, and noticed that he was moving quickly, as if panicking. The natural next move was to question all the landlords and pub staff near to the playing fields.

The two girls had had a few drinks at the *Commercial Inn* and the landlord was asked if he had noticed them being bothered or approached by any men. He had not, but after a while other local enquiries picked up several mentions of a young man who had come to watch the police and to watch the body being taken away. Several people had noticed him: that he was agitated and was always brushing hair away from his face. When details of him were put to the landlord, he confirmed that he had seen such a man on the night Pamela was killed, and that he had been drinking heavily.

That little detail of him constantly touching his hair was the detail that led to the man being noticed, and he turned out to be

Ovenden Way today. Ainley lived on here, about ten minute's walk from the Commercial. The author

Michael Ainley, a married man living in Ovenden way. He had a wife and two children, and his house was close to the playground –only a few hundred yards. Other people saw this movement of the hand on the hair, and it was enough to make him stand out.

Everything pointed to his guilt, but he took some time to crack, despite the fact that he was clearly nervous as soon as he was questioned, reacting sharply to plain, direct questions of fact. Ainley even denied seeing Pamela's picture in the paper, and it was noted that he read the *Daily Mirror,* which had carried a main feature on the killing. Perhaps most suspicious was the fact that he had scratches on his face, which he tried to explain by claiming he was caught by a bush along the roadside late in the dark. He kept telling the story that he had taken his wife out on that Saturday night, but when he was told that he had been seen out alone that night, he finally gave in, much distressed over what he had done. He said that he 'just saw red' and that he had dragged her into the field but 'she was a plucky little thing... she fought like a tiger. Then I realised she had seen me and could recognise me...'

Of course, he had to kill her then. His story to the police was that he saw her alone and it was a quiet area. The old maxim about crime, that 'I could do it, so I DID do it' applies most prominently here. He chatted her up, and she told him to leave her alone. Pamela pushed him away so he reacted by dragging her into the field. But when found she was almost totally naked; as the lawyer, D J Clarkson said at the trial, Pamela had been bitten repeatedly on her right breast and abdomen... there were indications that she had been held around the neck by her attacker...' All in all, this was a horrendous, cruel murder of a young woman who had simply enjoyed a quiet night out with a friend.

Ainley had been forthright about the main reason: that she recognised him. Later he wrote to her parents to express his emotions of sheer disgust at what he had done. What strikes the modern reader most about this case is the impressive thoroughness of the police and the sharp professionalism involved in moving so quickly and efficiently to the main suspect, despite the red herring of bloodstains found along a nearby street-marks which were most likely leaks from a parcel of meat.

The true horror of the murder must have been perceived most nakedly and disturbingly by the unfortunate man walking his dog on that apparently peaceful Sunday morning when this dreadful murder first became known. It also reinforces the common observation about the frequency of the perpetrator's return to the scene of the crime as the sign of guilt and a hint for the forces of law how they should act. The ultimate irony of the story is that the girl was attacked in such a public place; this confirms yet again the fact that paradoxically, sometimes open spaces are the most lonely of all, often away from hearing or available assistance.

CHAPTER 50

The Ripper on the Park
1979

T he story of Peter Sutcliffe's long reign of terror throughout West Yorkshire in the years 1975–80 has been well documented, and there is a growing library of works analysing his complex life-experience and psychological profile. In terms of the hunt for him by a huge team of officers and support staff in these years, the murder he committed in Halifax relates to two of the notable turns in the chase for this sadistic killer: the 'Ripper Tape' and the switch from prostitute to other, general female victims.

The Yorkshire Ripper murders offer the reader and historian a series of crime which relate vividly to the topography and cultural aspects of the West Riding sense of place and identity. The scenarios of the crimes he committed are almost stereotypes of 'The North' as represented in the popular media: killings in timber yards, dark alleys, unlit fields, red light districts: murders initially of people living on the fringe, only just keep their heads above water in a tough, unrelenting world driven by money and success. His murder in Halifax was entirely in keeping with this, as the town has almost infinite possibilities for concealment, surprise and entrapment when these things are in a killer's mind.

The bus stop on the edge of Savile Park, where Sutcliffe's victim was found.
The author

Before Sutcliffe actually committed murder in the town, he had 'practised' – or failed, whichever way ones sees it, and one of his early failures had been in Halifax. This had been a vicious attack on forty-six year old Olive Smelt in Boothtown. He had only just before this attacked Anna Rogulskyj in Keighley and now he ventured into Calderdale. Mrs Smelt, an office cleaner, had been out for a night with her women-friends and was given a lift home by a man she knew; she was dropped off in a Boothtown Road lay-by, with not far to walk home.

She had planned to take some fish and chips home to share with her husband, and decided to take a short-cut through an alley. This was almost a fatal error. Amazingly, it is recorded that the man who tried to kill her made a remark about the bad weather just seconds before she was dealt a crushing blow on the head which led one policeman to say that her skull was cracked 'like an egg-shell.' Olive Smelt was very lucky to survive that attack; she cried for help and managed to crawl. People nearby took her in, and emergency services called. She was taken to Leeds Infirmary, and eventually survived.

Everything in the attack had the same features as the assault on Mrs Rogulskyj: the clothes pulled up, random slash-marks on the back, and a handbag near, with nothing taken. This was to be a basic pattern, much more extreme and frenzied in the actual murders later in the series of killings and near-attempts. Undoubtedly, Olive Smelt, despite the awful depression and serious effects on all areas of her life which followed this, was amazingly still alive to tell the tale.

The Halifax murder was of Josephine Whitaker, on 4 April 1979. She had been on one of her regular visits to her grandparents, and the walk home entailed crossing the open parkland of Savile Park. This is so broad that the central areas present criminals with stretches of space in which their deeds would be indistinguishable and beyond any clear perception from the fringes or the roads. Many roads provide the borders between two areas of Savile Park, and one in particular is a busy road linking King Cross with the area around the hospital and Bell Hall. Between the junction where stands St Jude's church and the ends of the road which extends towards Wainhouse Folly, Josephine was killed, and her body found not far from a bus-stop by the road along the Savile Park housing.

The car park on Bull Green, where several people reported seeing a man in a car / carrying a hammer, at the time of the Yorkshire Ripper activities in the Halifax area. The author

Josephine was in the habit of walking to visit her grandparents who lived by the side of the busy Halifax to Huddersfield road, and was walking back home to her home in one of the terraced streets off Savile Park. It was a long walk, up-hill, but she was a tall, athletic girl. Ironically, she had received a new silver watch that day, ordered from a catalogue, and as she walked on the lonely place, she was asked the time, but the question was from the Yorkshire Ripper, and just seconds later, he had murdered the girl. She had waited late at her grandparents' house, waiting for her grandmother who had been to church, and it seemed rash to set off on that walk at eleven at night. The last thing her grandmother had said to her was 'take care.'

It later emerged that Sutcliffe was fond of being in the Halifax area, notably enjoying his drinking at the *Bull's Head* in the town. After all, four years had passed since he had attacked Olive Smelt. It is certain, then, that he knew the town well, and had clearly driven around the streets, noting the areas which would be perfect places for attack. In both Halifax cases, he had appeared quickly, from the shadows, attacked swiftly, and gone into the frenzy of mutilation which became his hallmark.

This murder was indicative of several things which were leading the police closer to Sutcliffe, after he had switched from attacking women in red light districts; one of the main elements was the time of the killing, as Josephine, a clerk with the Halifax Building Society, was murdered at 11.30 p.m. Several other killings had occurred at times in which the suggestion was that the killer was timing his journey home; the epicentre of all the murders was Bradford, in this sense. The attacks in Huddersfield, for instance, fitted in with these timings approximately. But by the time this was worked out, Sutcliffe had been caught, and this time it was in Sheffield, and he was charged at Hammerton Road police station.

The Halifax murder was entirely typical of his methods. It was in the dark, in a situation in which he could approach the victim from behind with the trademark hammer. It was not in defensible space, and as so often before in his assaults, it was on the fringe of housing. Just across the road from that corner of the park there are dwellings facing the park and then streets of terraces behind them. This tendency to be at his awful work only minutes away from ordinary domestic life explains how the paranoia and local myths generate.

In the case of Halifax, at the time of the killings, there were indeed several reported sightings of men in peculiar attire, and loitering with intent. People were looking with suspicion at their neighbours, as the media hype was so intense and full of the characteristic 'moral panic' of crime reporting. For example, people reported seeing a man dressed as a woman, and carrying a knife, in the car park next to the roundabout at Bull Green.

With hindsight, of course, it is easy to see why he chose the Savile Park area. It wasn't simply that it provided the open space and the lack of any crowd around; it was also that there are no public houses or clubs nearby. He was at this point in his nefarious career interested in preying on any lone female, and now it was starting to be young women taking risks by walking in dark places where their cries could not be heard. It was later than the 'dog-walking time' also, of course, when he struck. The next killing was a student in Bradford (Barbara Leach) and the circumstances were similar, as was the killing of Marguerite Walls in 1980 who was walking home late at night (a distance of a mile and thus vulnerable at several points in the journey) when he attacked her in a street of suburban Leeds.

As with all such truly terrible crimes, this attack in suburban middle class Halifax, at a site associated more with local football matches and equestrian events, there remains somehow a sort of tainted feel to the spot on the grass where Sutcliffe struck, and the account of how and where he killed only adds to the vulnerability of even the most close and comfortable communities.

Sources

Books
1. Roger Boar and Nigel Blundell, *The World's Most Infamous Murders* (Octopus) 1983.
2. Roger Cross, *The Yorkshire Ripper*, (Harper Collins) 1995.
3. Steve Fielding, *The Hangman's Record, 1868–1899* (Chancery House) 1994.
4. John A Hargreaves, *Halifax, A Photographic History of Your Town* (Black House/Smiths) 2002.
5. David T Hawkings, *Criminal Ancestors*, (Sutton) 1992.
6. Peter Thomas, *Mill, Murder and Railway* (Peter Thomas) 1973.
7. J Horsfall Turner, *Biographia Halifaxiensis*, printed for compiler, 1883.

Journals
Thoresby Society Miscellany, Vol. 8, 1998.
Transactions of the Halifax Antiquarian Society, 1910.

Ephemera
The Halifax Guardian Almanac, 1898–1930.

Index